Daring Do's

Daring Do's

A History of Extraordinary Hair

Mary Trasko

Flammarion

Paris - New York

Acknowledgments

Many people have aided and encouraged me in the preparation of this book, suggesting a passage from a lady's memoir, remembering a line from a poem or an astonishing photograph of a hairstyle. My warmest thanks to all who contributed over the past five years. I am grateful to Jane and John Stubbs for providing so many illustrations from their marvelous collection of books and prints, and for providing inspirations from the beginning of the project. Also, to C. J. Scheiner in New York for lending illustrations. I am indebted to Ruben Toledo and to Henry Koehler for allowing me to reproduce their original drawings. Many thanks to Horst for permision to include the photograph of Daisy Fellowes, and to all the photo archives, estates, and museum collections who kindly lent permissions. Thanks to Simon Doonan and Steven Johanknecht of Barneys New York for allowing me to photograph a few of the amazing wigs from the display treasure trove; and to RuPaul and to Monica Lynch of Tommy Boy Records for permission to reproduce the RuPaul photograph. Many, many thanks to all the photographers, stylists, and models who contributed, especially Josef Astor and Neal Barr, as well as Mathu Andersen, Sam and Carol Brown, Paul Edwards, Robert Grace, Karl Lagerfeld, Darrel Lane, Gwynnis Mosby, and Teresa Stewart. I am eternally grateful to the hairdressers who created the fantasy do's for the postscript—those who braided and threaded for hours, shaped gelatinized hair, balanced burning candles in wigs, wove tiny, shell-encrusted fishnets and coiffed mermaids, namely John D'Orazio, Veron Charles, Danilo, Julien d'Ys, Joan Gardner and Sally Kamara of MJ's Unisex, Orlando Pita, Ruth Sinclair, and Kerry Warn. My sincere thanks to those who kindly read and advised upon the text, especially Barbara Porter, for reading the section on ancient Egypt. I would like to gratefully acknowledge the authors of the many books on hairdressing, fashion and other subjects that I have cited, and to thank the staffs of the New York Public Library, the Center for Film Study in Los Angeles, and the Bibliotheque des Arts Décoratifs in Paris—all have given valuable assistance. I so appreciate the miracles Christa Weil worked with the text, and the spirited, sophisticated design for the book conceived by Jean-Philippe Gauvin and Dominic Smets. A million thanks to Diana Groven and Anne-Isabelle Vannier at Flammarion, and to Bartholémy de Lesseps for his translation of the text for the French edition. Others who have been most helpful: Susanne Bartsch, Gray Davis, Olivier des Clers de Beaumets, Amy Fine Collins, Nancy Kahan, Stacy Leigh, Christian Louboutin, Angela Miller, Rolando Niella, Fabienne Schwalbe, and Bpo Vigneron. Warmest thanks to my mother, Janina Trasko, for her reminiscences and recipes, and to Leo and Len Trasko. Three of my closest friends have provided immeasurable support: a million thanks to Isabelle Bosquet for her innumerable consultations, to Antonio da Motta Leal for such witty and wondrous illustrations, and to Stephen Szcze-panek for encouraging me to undertake the project, for contributing the illustration of Pierre Toussaint, and for countless ins-pirations, not the least of which is another great book title. I am greatly indebted to Will Schwalbe and Paula Litzky for being links in the chain that led me to Flammarion. And most of all to my editor, Suzanne Tise, who took on the project, who uncovered so much marvelous material for the book, and then brought it all together so stunningly.　　　　M.T.

Designed by Jean-Philippe Gauvin and Dominic Smets
Copyediting by Christa Weil
Index compiled by Emily Wanger
Typesetting by Octavo Editions, Paris
Photoengraving by Pack Edit, Paris
Printed and bound by Mame, Tours

Flammarion 26, Rue Racine, 75006 Paris

ISBN: 2-08013-549-X
Numéro d'édition: 0839
Dépôt légal: October 1994
Printed in France

Contents

Throughout much of history, the fashionable head of hair could not be farther from what we admire today. The styles of the past—wired, gummed, padded, powdered—look contrived, cumbersome, and, worst of all, unwashed. Thanks to eyewitness accounts and depictions of trends in hair fashion, we can see what could hardly be imagined, and be reminded once again that the pursuit of beauty has been a long road paved with frivolity and excess.

The height of lavishness and absurdity in coiffures was achieved in the arrangements of the 1770s, when noblewomen bedecked their heads with tall ships and allegorical panoramas, securings the arrangements with a plaster made of beef tallow or lard. These colossal headdresses disappeared with barely a trace, as if they existed in a realm of dreams. Why did none survive their time? The odor of the ageing arrangements was such that throwing them away was the only option, leaving a lovely assortment of props and combs, style in this case being truly fleeting.

Hairstyles offer rich revelations about the lives of women and their societies. In the 1920s, when women began cutting their long hair, it was an act of liberation. Religious and social establishments were duly outraged, and as one historian of the period has observed, "When one reads the spate of impassioned prose directed against these two styles of coiffure by the clergy of all denominations, one would think that bobbing and shingling were pseudonyms for the penchants of Sodom and Gomorrah."[1]

The ensnaring, frightening effect of living hair was frequently evoked in turn-of-the-century painting and photography.

Left: French caricature, c. 1775.

Women's hair has always provoked strong reactions. At one extreme are the fetishists who fantasize about stroking long, silky hair or who thrill at the thought of it caressing their body. Then there are those who are disgusted by the sight of a single hair on the bathroom floor or who find the experience of brushing up against a stranger's hair repulsive. The Surrealists recognized this dichotomy, and used hair in some of their most jarring works. Meret Oppenheim's *Fur Teacup*, for example, plays upon the revulsion elicited by hair cropping up where it does not belong. In contrast, the idea that a woman's hair could be vicariously arousing has led some cultures to hide it away. Yet once concealed, hair becomes highly eroticized.

We have grown so used to seeing women stretched naked across billboards that we can hardly imagine that in a time not so long ago modesty demanded that a woman's hair be covered in the Western world as well. Even at the turn of this

A. Grevin,
A Hair Fetishist,
c. 1900.

century, it was improper for a lady to appear without a hat or some type of head covering, not only in church, but on the street. All sorts of confiners and metal frames were patented to get the abundant tresses that women possessed under control, and to lessen the hair's tantalizing draw.

In eighteenth-century England, the young Lord Petre initiated a scandal when he mischievously snipped off a lock from the hair of Miss Arabella Fermor. The Fermor family viewed this as an utter violation. A friend, wishing to end the prolonged estrangement between the two families, asked Alexander Pope, the foremost satiric poet of his day, to write a poem that might put an end to the feud. Pope's mock-epic masterpiece, *The Rape of the Lock*, wittily admonishes "What dire offence from am'rous causes springs, / What mighty contests rise from trivial things, . . . Say what strange motive, goddess! could compel / A well-bred lord t'assault a gentle belle?"[2] The assault certainly seems trivial by today's stan-

dards, but in its day, the scandal titillated imaginations. A small printing of the poem was issued in 1712, but when a larger commercial printing was offered in 1714, the poem sold three thousand copies in four days![3]

Pope surmised that perhaps the young lord had merely fallen prey to the irresistible lure of the lock: "Fair tresses man's imperial race insnare, / And beauty draws us with a single hair."[4] Indeed, men have always been bewitched by the satiny gloss and luxurious abundance of long hair. The poems of Ovid catalogue in vivid detail the multitude of hairstyles in ancient Rome, but he makes it clear that what he really found captivating was the simplicity of the wind-blown Ariadne with her "blond hair streaming loose."[5] He writes rapturously about running his hands though his lover's hair: "What I did (no excuses!) was mess up / Her new coiffure. Like that, in disarray, / It looked splendidly windswept. Oh, her beauty—like / Atalanta's."[6]

Unlike the deadly Gorgon of ancient Greek myths, whose hideous face and snaked hair had the power of turning all who looked upon her into stone, this Pre-Raphaelite Medusa seduces with the terrible beauty of her gaze and the sensuality of her flowing tresses.
Anthony Frederick Sandys, Medusa, *1875.*

From ancient times to the French Revolution, court nobility set hairstyling trends. In a letter to her daughter in March of 1671, Madame de Sévigné proclaimed a new tousled look, just introduced by the duchesse de Ventadour in Paris, "the most ridiculous hairstyle you can imagine. And you can believe me, for you know how I love fashion."[7] Yet a short while later, she urged her daughter to adopt the very same ridiculous style, noting that her daughter's present "do" had become "out of the question." Fashion *mattered*, and even the slightest modification was reported as news. Although new styles were often only minute alterations of the old, a trend was usually discernible. The style soon became more and more exaggerated, until every variation had been attempted; then a silhouette as different as possible from the last style would be adopted and the process began again, as occurs right up to the present day.

From our perspective, it is difficult to fathom the amount of time that women who aspired to elegance spent on hairstyling. As late as the 1920s, Antoine, one of the most chic coiffeurs working in Paris, explained that it was not at all unusual among the "ultra-smart women" to have their hair done three times a day! The Duchess of Windsor was one of these ladies. Here Antoine describes her daily hairdressing regime: "In the morning for a little hat, something quite simple; in the afternoon perhaps to go to the races; in the evening, for formal use, perhaps with a little ornament. This does not mean the ordinary woman's several-times-a-day hair comb. It means a complete hairdressing by a coiffeur or maid."[8]

Daring Do's concentrates almost exclusively on feminine hairdressing because women's hair inspired the most magnificent flights of fantasy throughout history. Some men's styles extraordinary enough to merit inclusion serve as a counterpoint, proving that an obsession with hairstyling was by no means a feminine folly. One of the most extravagant

9

Rossetti's enraptured Delia dreams in ecstasy of the return of her husband. Her loose hair and meditative expression reflect the Victorian ideal of holy feminity. Dante Gabriel Rossetti, Miss E. Siddal.

ages of wig-wearing, the seventeenth and eighteenth centuries, was in fact ushered in by men. The costly, massive wigs worn by noblemen became a sign of social prominence and gave rise to the term "bigwig." There have always been men whose preoccupations with their hair were just as extravagant, if not more, than any woman's. Ludwig II, the "Mad King" who built such splendidly kitschy palaces in Bavaria in the late nineteenth century, could not enjoy his food unless his hair had been curled. In the 1920s, while many women were still agonizing over the decision of "to bob or not to bob," Stephen Tennant, one of the most fashionable young men in London, had his hair not only bobbed, but finger-waved and dusted with gold.

While barber shops have existed since ancient times, there was no equivalent for women until the late 1800s. With the emergence of a line of artist-hairdressers in seventeenth-century France, women summoned them or servants to

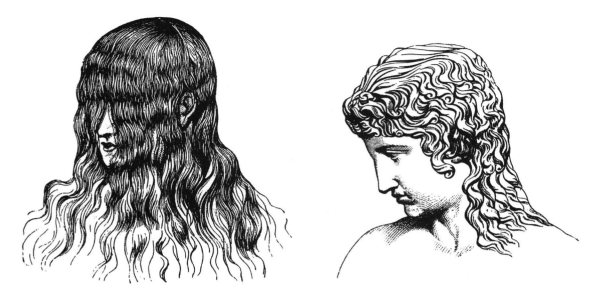

set their hair. Another possibility at court was for ladies of equal rank to style each other's hair, a social activity that provided a break from the rigorous court etiquette. Like so many other aspects of women's lives, this ritual took place behind closed doors. While paintings, drawings, caricatures, and other images present a vast recorded history of hairdressing, for the most part the stylists are unknown. Like today, most practitioners made their contributions with little or no recognition.

The freedom and power contemporary women have to shape their own destinies and appearances is truly unprecedented. Today the word "coiffure" seems antiquated, implying a degree of fuss that most women no longer tolerate. Women do not have time for coiffures; they get haircuts. Some readers may find it pathetic that women in the past spent hours having some intricate tableau styled into their hair, in hopes of eliciting praise or notoriety. But for

better or worse, fashion was where a woman of wealth could channel her creativity, and her less well-off sisters followed her example as best they could.

The master coiffeur Alexandre once described his art "as a desperate search for an eternal and fugitive beauty . . . the search for that which will last only for one day."[9] This book celebrates the time when coiffure, in all its frivolous, time-consuming glory, was still a major part of women's elegance and of the erotic game; when ladies and their hairdressers spent hours to achieve something remarkable.

Now women have much more important things to consume their days than the placement of ribbons and bows; still, it is fascinating to look back at the countless toilettes—where so many women spent their mornings and their evenings, gossiping and laughing, curling and setting, for the amusement of themselves and for the pleasure of others.

The bust of the elegant Plautilla, wife of Caracalla, had a removable marble wig that could be changed so that her portrait was never out of fashion.

Ancient Artifice

mages from vases, frescoes, and sculpture reveal remarkable similarities between the hairstyles of the ancient world and those closer to our day. There is virtually no difference between the short, wavy hair worn by the Roman empress Faustina the Elder in the second century A.D. and the finger-waved styles worn by the society beauties Sir Cecil Beaton photographed in the 1920s. We can visualize more clearly the tightly-plaited wigs of the ancient Egyptians by looking at some of the most popular black hairstyles today: cornrows and dreadlocks reinterpreted from traditional African techniques.

But the ancients also had proclivities we might consider bizarre. The Egyptians favored an adornment that looks like a party hat, but was actually a cone of perfumed fat which scented their wigs and their shoulders. These cones were considered deliciously sensual, one of their culture's most civilized pleasures. In Imperial Rome, people believed that the spirit guarding the head was gravely disturbed by washing the hair. Plutarch recommended performing this task only once a year—on 13 August, the birthday of the goddess Diana.[1]

The timeless quality of ancient styles is confirmed by their periodic revival right up to the present. The age-old practice of catching the hair back in a net outlived the Roman Empire into medieval times, and again became fashionable in the late nineteenth century as a way to manage

waist-length or longer hair. Nets resurfaced next in the early 1940s, when millions of women copied Vivien Leigh's snooded hair in *Gone With the Wind*. After the French Revolution, when women sought a style drastically different from the towering coiffures of the aristocracy, they looked back to the short, relatively simple hairstyles from antiquity, which were considered more appropriate for the newly egalitarian French society (following this trend was only prudent—those who stuck with the tall powdered wigs, which had come to symbolize aristocratic decadence, did so at risk of losing their heads!). In the mid-nineteenth century, when the French realist painter Gustave Courbet called his long beard "Assyrian," he was caught up in the excitement over the newly unearthed archaeological discoveries at the ancient city of Nineveh.

These digs revealed a culture that from 1500 B.C. onward was renowned throughout the Middle East for its skills in cutting, curling, layering, and dyeing hair. One Assyrian innovation has lasted as long as the wheel. Both male and female nobles had their hair set in curls and ringlets by slaves using a fire-heated bar—the first curling iron, an implement that would soon spread throughout the ancient cultures. Artificial curls were not an Assyrian innovation, however. Centuries before, the Egyptians, creating locks for wigs, twisted hair around metal rods and coated it with beeswax. Another curling method, used in Egypt and other parts of Africa, was to wind the hair tightly around cane sticks, then cake it with mud, hemp, or clay. After drying in the sun, the clay shell and cane were removed, leaving masses of locks similar to the dreadlocks that are formed in much the same way in parts of Africa today.

Certain preoccupations with hair have not changed much over the millennia. Ancient Egyptian medical papyri contain recipes for lotions to fight baldness, creams to nourish the scalp, and dyes to cover gray hair.[2] Two thousand years ago,

Greek gentlemen preferred blondes. Finally, an absolute passion for wigs existed throughout ancient civilizations.

The Many-Splendored Wigs of Egypt

Egyptian nobles, like their counterparts ever after, knew that a sense of luxury and grandeur was essential to convey the prestige of their court. Adornment was vital, and both men and women were mad for wigs. Formed of neatly plaited braids or locks, they were worn not only on festive occasions but as part of the daily wardrobe. The wig-wearing habit spread to almost every level of society, except to priests and laborers. Some people had shaven heads underneath, a sign of nobility, but others wore wigs on top of their hair, almost like a hat. Wigs were dyed bright colors—copper red from henna or bright blue from indigo. Cleopatra, queen and legendary seductress, had a great variety of colored wigs; she wore them with magnificent jewelry and linen dresses shot through with gold threads. Precious wigs were interred with their dead owners as a status symbol for the next world; one wig, discovered in a tomb dating from about 600 B.C., was made of pure silver.[3] (Apparently, an impressive wig was more important than a comfortable one when looking ahead to the next life!)

Most people owned at least one hairpiece, so wigmaking was an important activity. From the New Kingdom (c. 1550–1070 B.C.) onward, they were made from human hair. Earlier, animal hair, or a vegetable fiber (such as palm leaf or cotton) was used. A wigmaking studio excavated at Deir el Bahri revealed how the Egyptians made wigs more than three thousand years ago: a mixture of warm beeswax and resin was used to adhere curls or braids to a mesh cap woven from tightly plaited hair.[4]

The reason why wigs were so popular under the simmering Egyptian sun remains a mystery. A

A detail from the back of the throne of Tutankhamen (reigned 1361–52 B.C.) features the royal couple wearing short, tightly plaited wigs dyed indigo blue.

light fibrous wig, like a palm leaf creation, would certainly shade the head and have a cooling effect almost like a straw hat, but a wig made from dense braids, ornamented and coated with beeswax, must have been stifling.

Sometimes a woman's own hair was plaited. The braids were intertwined with colored ribbons and flowers, especially the lotus, which symbolized abundance. Over the braids, a circlet of gold mesh, decorated with lapis, turquoise, or colored glass, was tied onto the hair with a ribbon or else fastened with a chinstrap.

Inscriptions from the Old Kingdom (c. 2650–2150 B.C.) suggest that the hairdresser held an esteemed position, and that men usually performed the role. In the Middle and New Kingdoms, however, the hairdresser is invariably depicted as female.[5] In some cases, the stylist is rendered in a very small scale, barely the height of the long wig, indicating that slaves carried out the intricate and laborious braiding. Some carved

scenes evoke a simultaneity of events, suggesting that a noblewoman's toilette was very social—while her hair was plaited and perfumed, friends visited, children played, singers and musicians performed. During the toilette, women are shown bare-breasted, with their lower bodies wrapped in a kilt or skirt similar to what men wore.

Egyptian pictorial representations were idealized, and therefore can be misleading. Women, for instance, are almost always depicted as young, slender, and statuesque; the aim in temple and funerary art was to represent the ideal. The Egyptians carefully controlled how they would be perceived by their own people and later generations, but as long as one recognizes these biases, the period offers a wealth of revealing material about hairdressing.

At least three types of hair plaiting are discernible on both sexes: finely-woven braids; spiral curls; and long, crimped locks; all falling from a center part, twisted at the ends, and dipped in beeswax. It is difficult to establish with any certainty where these styles came from, but it is safe to say that hairdressing in Egypt and that in other African cultures shared a common root. Important features of Egyptian culture and dress originated in other parts of Africa; influences from Asia and the Near East had an impact as well. There is evidence that in the New Kingdom, the Egyptian rulers were polygamous and married foreign princesses. At least some women among the nobility were black. Noblewomen from other parts of Africa could have regularly introduced plaiting techniques from their homelands to the women of the Egyptian court—just as foreign princesses occasionally set new trends in the European courts in more recent times.

Beyond a doubt the Egyptians were great sensualists. Hairdressing was part of an eroticized, or at least highly pleasurable, toilette. This regimen included a daily soak in a fizzy bath of calcium carbonate and a wash with a detergent made from clay and ashes. The bath was often followed by a massage. Women buffed their bodies with sand and pumice until they were smooth and hairless, then applied fragrant creams and oils. Both women and men wore jewelry, makeup, and sometimes tattoos. They lined their eyes with kohl, and painted their faces with a white foundation made from lead carbonate and egg whites. (Derivatives of lead were commonly used in recipes for face painting, powdering, and hair lightening in many cultures, resulting in countless premature deaths and birth defects until its dangers were finally recognized in the mid-eighteenth century.) The elegant Egyptian's dressing table was covered with pots and bottles containing scents such as myrrh, saffron, frankincense, and a precious perfume extracted from acacia and teak seeds. Poet and author Diane Ackerman has described how the Egyptians discovered the *enfleurage* technique, which consisted of pressing aromatics into fatty oils, and created a wide variety of beautiful glass vessels to keep them.[6]

This love of fragrance carried through to hair-dressing. Ackerman muses, "An ancient Egyptian socialite attending a party would wear a wax cone of unguent on the top of her head; it would melt slowly, covering her face and shoulders with a trickle of perfumed syrup. It probably felt as if small beetles were crawling all over her, pushing balls of fragrance."[7] Scenes of social gatherings show musicians and servants wearing these cones as well. Typically, they were formed from goose or ox tallow impregnated with myrrh. They provided not only a pleasurable experience, but a balm to counter the drying effect of the sun.

In another curious practice, both royal women and men wore stylized false beards on ceremonial occasions. Curled, scented, and sometimes woven with gold braids, they were like a hairpiece for the chin. These beards symbolized a link to the gods, or to kings, who were thought to descend from the gods. For women, the beard had another advantage: within the male-dominated power structure, the more masculine attributes she possessed, the better. Gay Robins observes that women did not easily occupy the Egyptian throne; in nearly three millennia, only four out of two or three hundred rulers were female.[8] Hatshepsut, however, ruled for more than ten years, possibly twenty, during which time she developed diplomatic and trade links with other countries and built and restored monuments, among other achievements. It is not known whether she dressed as a man in real life, but she wore a false beard to symbolize her authority, and ordered that she be represented on monuments without breasts, in the male costume of a warrior.[9]

Among the full-wigged silhouettes, distinct looks coincided with important passages in life. Married women are often depicted wearing one of two styles: with a handful of locks falling forward on each shoulder and the rest falling behind, or in an enveloping wig in which the

*Elegant chignons held back with
diadems, ribbons, or decorative scarves were
the preferred hairstyle for
the women of the Hellenistic period.*

hair hangs fully around the shoulders without any division. Children had shaved heads with one curled lock falling on the right temple, which explains why the hieroglyph for "child" is a stylized curl.

Because the Egyptians idealized their representations, all the glorious eccentricities that must have existed are lost to us. We can only imagine the extravagant do's that might have been worn by the "style rebels," those individuals from every age who prefer not to look like everyone else. Hairstylists working today, interpreting traditional African methods of plaiting and threading the hair, suggest the infinite possibilities.

The Fragrant and Divine Curls of Ancient Greece

During the golden age of the fifth century B.C., Greek society was dominated by an ethos of masculinity and ruggedness. The male was the perfect ideal of beauty, especially a man with a head full of curls. Even though the Greeks favored a natural appearance, the irrepressible instinct for adornment manifested itself in their shapely curls and in the floral wreaths worn by both sexes. Dinner guests were presented with crowns woven from ivy and myrtle. Around 90 B.C. the poet Meleager wrote of his ravishing Heliodora, "I shall plait white violets, I shall plait the soft narcissus, together with myrtle-berries, and I shall plait the laughing lilies and sweet crocus . . . so that the garland on the temples of Heliodora with the perfumed curls shall wreathe with flowers her beautiful cascade of hair."[10]

Athenian women combed their hair into a heavy chignon, held in place by long hairpins of gold and ivory, or drew it back in a net that sometimes was attached to bands that passed around the forehead. Spartan women preferred a ponytail threaded through with beads or pearls. In the first century A.D., enterprising Cypriots created a

toupee that quickly moved from their island to other cultures. It consisted of a wire frame worn ear-to-ear like a hairband, hung with an ornamental row of spiral locks.

What is most interesting among the Greeks, however, is not styling or ornamentation, but their early attempts at blonding; with them, we find the first reference in history to blond hair being more desirable for women than darker shades. The lighter color signified innocence, superior social standing, and sexual desirability (perhaps because of its rarity—most Greeks were dark-haired). The poet Anacreon wrote of "golden-haired Love."[11] Gods, goddesses, and great beauties like Helen of Troy were often depicted as golden-haired or fair-haired. Women lightened their hair by rinsing it in a potassium solution and rubbing it with a pomade of yellow flower petals and pollen. Men, too, dusted their hair with pollen and gold, but as the dramatist Menander noted in the fourth century B.C., they had a more permanent method:

"The sun's rays are the best means for lightening the hair, as our men well know. . . . After washing their hair with a special ointment made in Athens, they sit bareheaded in the sun by the hour, waiting for their hair to turn a beautiful golden blond. And it does."[12] Another mixture was concocted from harsh soaps and alkaline bleaches from Phoenicia, then the soap center of the Mediterranean. These crude concoctions often failed to produce the desired hair color, so the Greeks either wore wigs or powdered their hair, the preferred colors being gold, silvery white, or red.

In ancient Greece, a woman's hair could be a crown or a badge of servitude, even of shame. In the Doric period, a bride cut her hair on the day of her marriage as a sign of humility and a renunciation of personal vanity. A jealous husband who doubted the fidelity of his wife would not hesitate to shave her head to rob her of her beauty and to keep her from going out. Women were chattel, totally subordinate to men. In the civilizations of

the ancient world, Greek women seemed to have had one of the least fortunate lots.

Roman Tantrums and Tresses

The difference in the lifestyles of Greek and Roman women was dramatic. Roman women had some say in whom they married, they were literate, they could divorce. Roman society was permissive and progressive—the lifestyle of the aristocracy was as pleasure-seeking as that of the French aristocracy in the eighteenth century. It amused Messalina, wife of the emperor Claudius in the first century A.D., to prowl the brothels in a blond wig, which prostitutes were required by law to wear to denote their profession. When Messalina returned home without it, the wig was returned to her at the palace.[13] It is difficult to say what brought on the trend, but soon respectable ladies decided that yellow was a fashionable wig color, causing more than a bit of confusion! The

Both Martial and Juvenal describe the "orbis" hairstyle worn by first-century Roman women, in which the hair was brushed forward and painstakingly crimped to form a massive edifice of tight curls.

The emperor Claudius's wife, the nymphomaniacal Messalina, is said to have donned a blond wig to visit Roman brothels.

empress Faustina the Elder, also notorious for her profligacy, loved the quick changes in appearance that wigs allowed. She collected them passionately, eventually amassing more than seven hundred wigs in every conceivable length and color.[14]

The variations in Roman coiffures were endless, as the poet Ovid observed: "Some need to keep it loose and windswept, / Others to pin it back; / Some like tortoiseshell combs, some prefer to brush it / Out in soft flowing waves—But you can't count all the acorns on an oak's branches, / or Hybla's bees, or wild beasts in the Alps, / And I can't be comprehensive about hair-fashions / When every day brings out a chic new style."[15] Roman fashions changed so quickly that sculptors commissioned to carve portraits busts were obliged to top them with detachable marble wigs, so that the likeness could be updated as rapidly as hairstyles changed.

Hair was set not only with tortoiseshell combs, but with long hairpins, hollow and gener-

ous enough to double as handy containers for perfume, or poison. Taking the technology of the wire-frame Cypriot toupees one step farther, corkscrew curls were dressed on tiara-like diadems, built up like a false-front facade. While these coiffures were demure compared with the truly towering styles of the eighteenth century, the difference between the high front and low back made them the subject of many jests. The poet and satirist Juvenal wrote: "So numerous are the tiers and stories piled upon one another on her head! In front you would take her for Andromache; She is not so tall behind; you would not think it was the same person."[16]

A men's hairdresser, or *tonsor*, attended to his clientele in a shop where he cut, curled, dyed, and perfumed their heads, and then, as a finishing touch, spread a bit of makeup on their cheeks. He even applied patches to cover blemishes, although the man who left wearing patches and scent was often ridiculed in the street. Ovid warned men against "torturing" their hair with curling irons, noting that a natural and rugged look was more fitting: "Real men / Shouldn't primp their good looks. When Theseus abducted / Ariadne / No pins held up his locks."[17]

Likewise, a woman had her *ornatrix*, a specially trained slave or servant adept at hairdressing and the particularly trying task of using a curling iron (in this case primitive tongs heated in a metal sheath under burning coals). She was only one among as many as two hundred slaves that attended to a Roman lady of high rank, each one being responsible for a particular aspect of her toilette—staining her eyebrows, scrubbing her teeth, anointing her with perfumes. A matron's behavior was rarely angelic toward any of her servants, but to the *ornatrix* many were absolute shrews. The matrons threw objects at their maids, beat them with hand mirrors, or worse. As Juvenal observes, "If Madame has an appointment and wished to be turned out more nicely than usual . . . the unhappy Psecas who does her hair will have her own hair torn, and the clothes stripped off her shoulders and breasts. 'Why is this curl standing up?' she asks, and then down comes a thong of bull's hide to inflict chastisement for the offending ringlet!"[18] And as the epigrammatist Martial relates, "One curl of the whole round of hair had gone astray, badly fixed by an insecure pin. This crime Lalage avenged with the mirror in which she had observed it and Plecusa, smitten, fell because of those savage locks."[19] Ovid chastises, "Don't vent your spleen on your lady's-maid: I detest a girl who / Claws the poor creature's face, or stabs / Her arm with a needle."[20]

He devotes an entire poem to chiding his lover about an unfortunate hairdressing experience; his verses could have been written yesterday, proving that hairdressing's attendant pleasures and agonies are truly timeless.

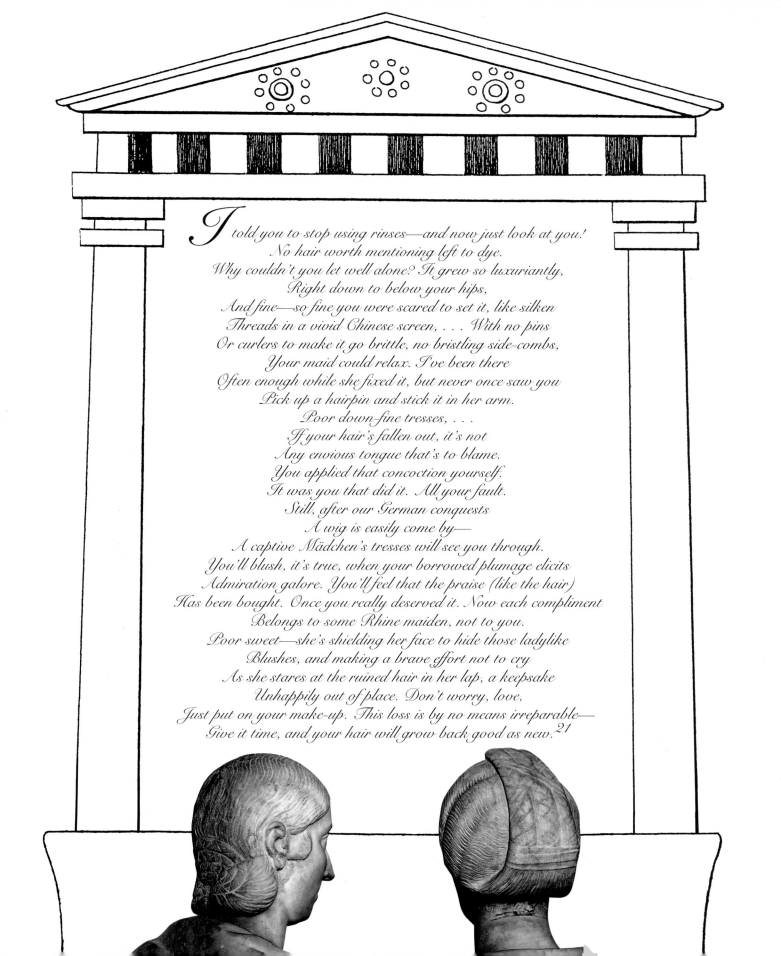

I told you to stop using rinses—and now just look at you!
No hair worth mentioning left to dye.
Why couldn't you let well alone? It grew so luxuriantly,
Right down to below your hips,
And fine—so fine you were scared to set it, like silken
Threads in a vivid Chinese screen, . . . With no pins
Or curlers to make it go brittle, no bristling side-combs,
Your maid could relax. I've been there
Often enough while she fixed it, but never once saw you
Pick up a hairpin and stick it in her arm.
Poor down-fine tresses, . . .
If your hair's fallen out, it's not
Any envious tongue that's to blame.
You applied that concoction yourself.
It was you that did it. All your fault.
Still, after our German conquests
A wig is easily come by—
A captive Mädchen's tresses will see you through.
You'll blush, it's true, when your borrowed plumage elicits
Admiration galore. You'll feel that the praise (like the hair)
Has been bought. Once you really deserved it. Now each compliment
Belongs to some Rhine maiden, not to you.
Poor sweet—she's shielding her face to hide those ladylike
Blushes, and making a brave effort not to cry
As she stares at the ruined hair in her lap, a keepsake
Unhappily out of place. Don't worry, love,
Just put on your make-up. This loss is by no means irreparable—
Give it time, and your hair will grow back good as new.[21]

In the 15th century, married women covered their hair with elaborate veils or turbans that assumed fantastic shapes: the hennin, or steepled headdress, and the extraordinary "butterfly" headdress of transparent gauze held up with long pins.

Petrus Christus,
Portrait of a Young
Woman, *15th century.*

After the Fall

Little written material on hairstyles or dressing techniques remains from the period spanning the Roman Empire's fall in the fifth century A.D. to the fourteenth century. The cosmetic recipes and cures that have survived—advice on preventing wrinkles, whitening the teeth, dyeing hair—were recorded in monasteries. Among the preserved wisdom: apply leeches to the skin to whiten it, and soften the hair by rubbing the scalp with the body of a lizard boiled in olive oil. (The lizard notwithstanding, the olive oil made better sense than many other treatments.)

In the medieval period, strange pointed headdresses and floating veils prevailed in many countries. The practice dated back to the second century A.D., when the Christian Church ordained that women cover their heads upon entering a place of worship, and to Middle-Eastern headdresses introduced by the Crusades. The decree

fostered a longstanding fashion for millinery of all sorts—turbans, hoods, bonnets, and the hennin, a cone-shaped hat. The hair was simply a foundation for the headdress, which was usually elaborately folded, embroidered, or encrusted with jewels. Women shaved their hairline and plucked their eyebrows to emphasize the allure of a high, expansive forehead. Hairpieces were uncommon, due to the Christian writers claiming, as they did in reference to so many other adornments, that they encouraged an unhealthy regard for personal vanity.

Despite the sanctions against its display, long hair continued to be prized, especially golden hair. An anonymous Greek verse from the thirteenth century praises one Chrysorrhoe: "Her tresses were like rivers, locks full of love; the hair on the maiden's head glowed and flashed brighter than the sun's golden rays."[22] By 1300 the story of Lady Godiva had passed into legend. Godiva, wife of Leofric, the lord of Coventry, pleaded with her

Jacopo Ligozzi, Head of a Woman, *16th century.*

husband to lessen the taxes on the townspeople. Aware of her extreme piety, he stated he would not relent unless she rode naked through the town. After issuing a proclamation that all people should remain indoors with their windows shut, Godiva rode her horse though the streets cloaked only in her long blond hair. Her husband kept his word and abolished the taxes.

With the rise of urban centers across Europe, a great many trade and artisanal guilds were established. The first public guild of barbers was registered in France in 1301, when hair-cutters banded together with cutters of another kind—surgeons! During the four centuries that the barber-surgeons' guild existed, there was constant feuding between the two groups, with each attempting to encroach upon the other's work while protecting its own. After much bickering, it was decided by decree that barbers were limited to pulling out teeth and blood-letting, and surgeons could not barber or shave. This struggle had a lasting impact, prompt-

ing doctors to long ignore problems of the hair and scalp. Hair remedies were left to peddlers and quacks who prescribed spurious treatments based on superstition.

The Eroticism of Cascading Tresses

Respectable married women living in Italy in the sixteenth century were expected to conceal their hair, perhaps allowing only a fugitive lock to catch an admiring glance. As Mary Rogers, a historian of representations of women in sixteenth-century Italian painting has explained, "That the covering, braiding, or other containment of women's hair after they were married . . . connoted a modest intention to signal unavailability and to mute the erotic impact of untrammelled locks was neatly conveyed by the author of a tract on the excellence of women of 1526: heads were kept covered to keep desire in check."[23] Virtuous women were advised not to spend too much time

Pisanello's depiction of the princess Trebizonde features one of the most admired beauty traits of the 15th century: a smooth, high forehead, achieved by plucking the hairline back several inches. The effect was further accentuated by pulling the hair up into a large basket-like construction held by ribbons or hairpieces, which showed off a long delicate neck.

29

*The flowing tresses of Botticelli's
virginal young women were enhanced
by elaborate hairpieces. Blond hair
was preferred by the elegant women
of Florence; Renaissance bleaching recipes
recommended such astonishing substances
as lizard grease and grilled bear bones.*

admiring their tresses in a mirror—this was considered dangerous and inciteful behavior as is attested to by the numerous *vanitas* paintings of the period.

Before a woman was married, however, she was free to display her hair, which was likely to be her most important physical asset. As Agnolo Firenzuola wrote in his dialogue of 1548, *Of the Beauty of Women*, "However well-favoured a lady may be if she have not fine hair, her beauty is despoiled of all charm and glory. . . . The hair should be fine and fair . . . now of gold, now of honey, and now of the bright and shining rays of the sun; waving, thick, abundant, and long."[24]

To achieve these honeyed highlights, women sat with their hair splayed out over the brim of a crownless hat, allowing the hair to become sunstreaked. Lucrezia Borgia, daughter of Pope Alexander VI, delayed her wedding procession an entire day just so her long, golden hair could be washed, dried, and properly arranged. Upon her arrival in Ferrara, the historian Christopher Hare

Piero di Cosimo, La Bella Simonetta, *c. 1480.*

In mid-16th-century England, neat hairstyles of small curls replaced veiled headgear.
The time required to achieve these styles helped bring wigs back into fashion.
Queen Elizabeth I is known to have possessed at least eighty.
Anonymous, Portrait of Elizabeth I, *16th century.*

relates, "Her head was covered with a net shining with gold and diamonds, under which her beautiful hair fell freely over her shoulders."[25]

Judging from the accounts of the day, men were completely enraptured by "golden-haired" women. No wonder women with graying hair and those who were dark-haired sometimes wore hairpieces created from white or yellow silk threads, so that an illusion of gold could be seen under their headdress. Rogers remarks that "Golden tresses tumbling loose, long, and free cast a potent erotic spell, being unfamiliar in contemporary women and connected with the alluring goddesses and sirens from the fantasy past of pagan antiquity or romance."[26]

Renaissance painters such as Botticelli and Titian painted high-born married ladies as Venuses or other allegorical figures, which allowed them to render their cascading hair without creating a scandal. When a lady was portrayed as herself, she was usually depicted with her hair

entwined in a dramatic arrangement, bound with ropes of gold chains or studded with pearls and jewels. Women of more modest means wove flowers into their hair, as Firenzuola explains, "Not all our peers have the wherewithal to attire themselves with the gems of the Orient . . . so it was needful to use the riches of our gardens."[27]

By 1550, the fashion of frizzing began in France, which involved heating the hair, if waves were desired, then teasing it for volume. The hair was then brushed over pads or wire frames to achieve the silhouette of the moment. These sculptured styles were held in place by gum mucilage, an expensive fixative available only to the upper classes. Women of lesser means copied the fashion as best they could, grounding a paste from rotten oak or flour. To compensate for the stickiness of the paste, the arrangement was dusted with powder. This marked an important transition: from wearing dramatic headdresses to the actual shaping of the hair itself. It brought

about many local variations. In Venice, a "bedeviling" mode developed of twisting the hair into two horns at the front of the head.

Wealth brought back from the New World had made Spain the major European power by 1550. In the second half of the sixteenth century, noblewomen throughout Europe adopted the Spanish court dress of high-necked, stiff bodices with cone-shaped skirts, and men and women alike were seen in ruff collars. Like so many elements of fashion, the ruff gradually grew to enormous size. It rose high at the back of the neck, calling for hairstyles that were short at the nape and high in front, which in turn encouraged the use of pads and gum.

In England, Elizabeth I came to the throne in 1558, a tall, red-haired, twenty-five-year-old who more than shared her age's passion for finery. Her two thousand dresses were of only the finest fabrics, many of them encrusted with jewels. She possessed at least eighty wigs, most of them in

reddish gold or saffron yellow. When it was time to sit for her portrait, she wore a reddish gold wig, or in her later years, a golden brown one. The magnificence of these portraits is breathtaking: her ruff or lace collar is extravagantly set with seed pearls, and her wig sparkles with an astonishing array of gemstones—large emeralds and rubies set in gold, sometimes forming a pendant with a chain of colossal pearls. Elizabeth understood well the importance of image in maintaining her power, and how sumptuous attire had reinforced the prestige of her court, lessons that would not be lost on Louis XIV in the next century.

The queen's ladies bought wigs and ornamented them as impressively as their fortunes allowed. This display of wealth and ostentation was novel, or at least in this period it was indulged to a novel degree. Previously, ladies of quality shrouded themselves in veils or head-dresses, seeking to conceal their charms, not to flaunt them. But Elizabeth's noblewomen were not interested in clothes that were modest or retiring. They dressed in fabrics heavy with seed pearls and painted the veins on their bosom blue to emphasize their aristocratic pallor. Coquettish beauty patches shaped like stars and half-moons littered their faces. These preoccupations prompted a gentleman of 1607, Thomas Tomkis, to crack, "A ship is sooner rigged by far, than a gentlewoman made ready."[28]

The frizzed, gummed hairstyles were so uncomfortable that most women gave up on them, preferring to shave their heads and wear a full wig instead. Even children wore wigs trimmed with expensive lace and feathers. But these hairpieces, laden with treasures, had their drawbacks. They brought about a rash of crime which left victims bereft of pride as well as property: wig snatching! Thieves would rip wigs off the heads of children in the street. They even schemed to cut holes in the backs of carriages—after the lady was seated inside, they would grab her wig and disappear!

"When your posterity shall see our pictures they shall think we were foolishly proud of our apparell" noted a gentleman named Foley in 1605, whose comment was preserved in religious records.[29] The Renaissance may have been coming to an end, but its sensibility, delighting in the pomp and drama of extraordinary pageants, courtly functions, theatrical events, and processions, would continue well into the baroque age. Its extraordinary hairstyles, built up on wire frames, padded and stuck with jewels, set a new standard in lavish adornment. Already, styling techniques were coming into practice that would make possible the grand and preposterous coiffures of the seventeenth and eighteenth centuries.

Two portraits of Marie de Medici flank one of the queen of Denmark and Norway, illustrating the royal fondness for hair bedecked with baubles.

Right: Nicholas Hilliard, A Noblewoman from the Court of Elizabeth I, *1590–95.*

Mlle des Faveurs à la Promenade à Londres.

Académie de coiffures, *1788*.

A Gallery of Extravagances

Coiffure in the most lavish decades of this period went beyond gilding the lily. It was more like the lily was gilded, pomaded, powdered, stuck with pins and plumes, and hung with bows. Never were more startling hair creations accepted as the fashionable norm. Portraits and letters of the day reveal such extravagances as a garden scene headdress complete with a spinning windmill and brook made from mirror shards. Clever ladies and their hairdressers dreamed up fantasies that were allegorical, topical, and, above all, huge. The hairdresser Baulard managed to construct in the 1770s a headdress *à la grand-mère* which could be collapsed by a full foot using concealed springs, in case the wearer encountered her grandmother, who was liable to faint away at the sight of a family member sporting this ludicrous fashion.

Many hours were given over to creating fabulous coiffures for women. The princesse de Machin once had her hair wrapped around the bars of a birdcage containing a colorful array of live butterflies. Ingenious foundations and artificial padding eventually elevated these constructions to an absurd altitude—three feet or even higher when adorned with feather plumes. In one of the many hairdressing caricatures from the 1770s, the decade of the most astounding hairworks, a coiffeur sets the curls at the summit of a towering arrangement while balancing atop a ladder. It was not possible for fashionable ladies to sit in a carriage without crouching, making even the shortest trips an exhausting ordeal.

37

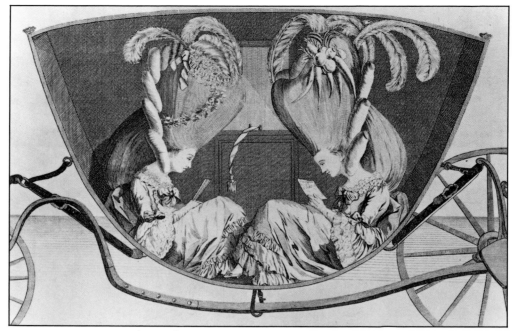

The Vis–à–Vis Bisected, or The Ladies Coop, *1776.*

Supporting such a load caused headaches and was, literally, a pain in the neck. One English noblewoman became a fashion victim in the gravest sense when her tall, fancifully styled wig brushed the flames of a sconce in the Bath Assembly rooms in 1776. The poor lady died of burns, but that did not keep the English satirists from immortalizing the event in verse:

> *Yet Miss at her rooms*
> *Must beware of her plumes,*
> *For if Vulcan her feather embraces,*
> *Like poor Lady Laycock,*
> *She'll burn like a haycock,*
> *And roast all the Loves and Graces.[1]*

There was an epidemic of near-fatal accidents—accounts tell of women and men with their hair aflame, knocking wigs off each other's heads or being doused with wine at dinner parties. Considering that all rooms, public and private, were illu-minated by burning candles, and that the wigs' silhouettes were continually changing, it is no wonder accidents were so commonplace.

These follies had their roots in the new hair-dressing techniques that became fashionable in the mid-seventeenth century. The standard fixative—gum paste—was replaced by a lard-based pomade. This held hair fast over a frame, allowing for ever grander and more elaborate styles. Pomades—in essence, solidified fat—had been commonly used in ancient times. But their revival in this era, in various cultural settings around the world, brought hairdressing into an entirely new realm of craftsmanship and artifice.

The pendulum of fashion swings fiercely and fully during these two centuries. During Louis XIV's reign, the king reproached court ladies for their *tours*, or towers of hair. Fifty years later, when Madame de Pompadour was the trendsetter at Versailles, arrangements were styled close to the head and discreetly accented with fresh flowers.

Le Stratagème amoureux, *c. 1770*.

*The ladies of the French
court dictated fashion throughout Europe.*

Louis XIV Surrounded by the Ladies of his Court,
from the Royal Almanach, 1667.

Finally, in Marie Antoinette's day, colossal and highly decorative constructions were once again in fashion. They toppled during the French Revolution, which spawned a reaction back to short-haired, natural styles.

Somersaults and Heartbreakers at Louis XIV's Court

By 1660 Louis XIV's court had wrested the mantle of fashion away from the Spanish nobility. The French now set the style in etiquette, fashion, decoration, and other pleasurable pursuits, and one of the pastimes in which ladies of the court indulged with particular zeal was coiffure. Louis himself acknowledged that hairstyle was a constant preoccupation and inexhaustible topic of conversation among them. Puffs of hair were built out over pads; ringlets sprang from a U-shaped wire fastened onto the head with hairpins. The curls draped over wires often slipped off, making it necessary for the

"For the women of my court,
hairstyle remains the most important thing,
the subject is inexhaustible."
—Louis XIV

lady to retreat and re-wire her coiffure. It was common for the longer hair in back to be covered with a cap or pulled back into a bun, leaving one long ringlet to cascade over the shoulder.

Elite circles were constantly christening new styles and flourishes. Innovations like *confidants* (small curls at the ears), *crève-coeurs* or heart-breakers (curls at the nape of the neck), and *favourites* (ringlets dangling from the side of the face) kept the curling irons hot. This capricious terminology, a complete mystery to the uniniti-ated, was essential to the snobbery of being *au courant*. In Boursault's comedy *Les Mots à la Mode*, a husband becomes enraged when he finds upon his wife's dressing table what appears to be a compromising note. His daughters arrive to assure him that it is, in fact, a bill from her hairdresser. No wonder that poor man was bewildered when he read, "Note of expenses in gallantry: for a somer-sault with a musketeer, plus a go-ahead and a squeeze-me-all-over: 800 francs."[2]

41

Ladies of the Spanish court preferred a horizontal hairstyle built out on wires.

The Spanish court had its own distinctive variation on the French hairstyle, depicted in the court portraits by Diego Velázquez. The hair of the infantas was plaited and built onto crescent-shaped forms, wide rather than tall to balance the width of their farthingales (wide, wire-hooped skirts). The horizontally-pronounced Spanish style was not drastically different from the French style, where the hair was built up vertically and the farthingale extended full all around. Yet when Infanta Maria Theresa arrived in France to marry Louis XIV in 1660, the French perceived a world of difference and criticized her mercilessly: "*Son habit était horrible*," the court ladies charged.[3] This put-down, her first taste of the intense rivalries at Europe's most fashionable court, was a shock for the infanta, whose homeland had until recently set the fashion with its splendid yet sober dress. Suddenly she was faced with lavish embroideries, ribbons, high-heeled shoes—and these on the men! Upon her marriage, Maria

Theresa became Queen Marie Thérèse and received a total makeover *à la Française.*

Earlier in seventeenth-century France a line of artistic hairdressers—the coiffeurs—had emerged, marking the beginning of professional hairstyling and of male dominance within it. The line began with a Monsieur Champagne, who was not only among the first, but also among the most audacious of hairdressers. Before him, only women had been allowed to work with women's hair; in 1605 the Catholic church threatened to excommunicate any woman who allowed a man to set it. But, as was so often the case when clergymen took on matters of fashion, the rulings were taken lightly.

Monsieur Champagne worked from 1635 until the 1650s, before the first brilliance of Louis XIV's court had dawned. After establishing his name in France, Champagne made at least one tour of the Scandinavian courts where he became the favorite coiffeur to Queen Christina of Sweden.

In his *Historiettes,* the society chronicler Tallemant des Réaux provided a rare portrait of the master at work: "This scoundrel, through his art in hairdressing and in pushing himself forward, was sought after and caressed by all the women. Their weakness for him was such that they put up with a hundred impertinences. Some he left with their hair only half done; to others, he refused after doing only one side of their hair, to finish the job if they did not kiss him."[4] Despite his insolence, or perhaps because of it, the court ladies worshiped Champagne. This clever rogue played an important role in establishing the hairdresser as a man of taste who created fashion. Soon hairdressers would be advising women on their makeup and on the placement of their beauty patches, an essential accessory in a time of rampant smallpox.

Following Champagne's lead, coiffeurs sought to distinguish themselves from barbers and wigmakers, who in the coiffeurs' opinion had only the most mechanical work, while they themselves

Fig. 3

Fig. 9

Fig. 16.

created beauty, fashion . . . art! The first hair-styling academies were not established until the next century, so those wishing to work as hairdressers apprenticed themselves to practicing coiffeurs, some of whom had only recently crossed over from other professions. Maids working in the service of noblewomen often had plenty of hairdressing knowledge and experience, but the coiffeurs claimed superiority, maintaining that they were responsible not only for reproducing current styles, but for setting trends. To announce and demonstrate their latest creations, they bestowed dolls with minutely-styled coiffures which were then displayed in public and passed among friends and relatives.

On 4 April 1671, the marquise de Sévigné wrote to her daughter, devoting several pages to a new coiffure, known as the *hurluberlu*, or "hurly-burly," a tousled look which involved setting the hair in curling papers. (This style was, in fact, created by a woman, Madame Martin, who remained for several years the favorite hairdresser to Louis XIV's court.) Madame de Sévigné, one of the great letter writers of the period, took pains to record not only events from social and literary life, but also such minute details as the latest hairstyles: "Imagine a head parted in the middle like a peasant to within two fingers of the pad. The hair is cut on each side, stage by stage, to form large round curls with a negligent air, which do not come any lower than one finger below the ear. It looks very young and very pretty, like two bouquets of hair on each side. . . . Ribbons are added in the ordinary way, and a large curl placed between the pad and the coiffure. . . . I do not know if I have represented this fashion very well for you: I'll have a doll's hair dressed to send to you."[5]

Although ceaselessly reworked and renamed, the court coiffures were remarkably similar at any given time as the whole court adopted *le dernier cri*, the only difference being the color of the ribbons, which were usually coordinated with the

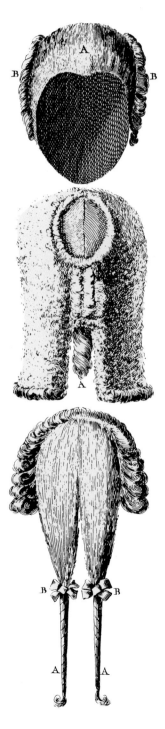

dress. Ribbons were popular accents with every-one from young girls to elderly dowager duchesses. One beribboned style came about quite by accident: the duchesse de Fontanges, a young favorite of the king, was riding with his hunting party when a branch tore loose a ribbon from her coiffure. Once it was retrieved, she swept her hair upward, tied it with the ribbon, *et voilà*! The king's admiration of her handiwork set off the rage for swept-up styles and hair ribbons *à la Fontanges*. The style was tremendously popular for more than a decade. Alas, after many modifications what had begun as a charming improvisation ended up an ungainly profusion of ribbons and wires.

Louis XIV understood well the value of dress as propaganda to spread the influence of his court. As Diana de Marly wrote in her book on the fashions of the period, "The Glory of the King had to be illustrated in cloth of gold and silver, and chains of diamonds. It is a wonder the ostrich did not become extinct, the demand for its plumes

was so great."[6] Early in Louis's reign, the English court had adopted the French fashions in all their extravagance. But after the publication of a score of pamphlets criticizing the effete French style, the English courtiers of Charles II began setting their own fashion trends. It upset Louis to think that the English would dare challenge his supremacy in matters of fashion. All the same, he himself tried out a few of the English fashions from time to time, helping to establish a dialogue and rivalry between the two courts.

The ostentation spreading from the courts through society was widely criticized by the clergy, including an English pastor by the name of Thomas Hall. In his treatise entitled *The Loathe-someness of Long Haire . . . with an Appendix against Painting, Spots, Naked Breasts, etc.* Hall made it clear that he had no tolerance for any such wanton display. This 1654 essay enumerates various Biblical references suggesting that long, perfumed locks were not what God intended for

men. He reserved his harshest criticism, however, for the newly fashionable feminine styles, noting with alarm "a most loathesome and horrible disease in the haire, unheard-of in former times, bred by modern luxury and excess. It seizeth specifically upon women, and by reason of a vicious venomous humour, glues together (as it were) the hair of the head with prodigiously ugly intanglement . . . full of nastiness, vermin, and noysome smell."[7] The ladies could hardly argue with the good pastor about the smell; lard-based pomades were usually scented with aromatic oils, but after a few days the fragrance evaporated, leaving only the smell of rancid fat.

Wondrous and Wooly
A Golden Age of Wigs

By 1665 French wigmakers were prospering enough to establish their own guild apart from the barber-surgeons. People of all classes and profes-

sions wore wigs. There were horsehair wigs which practically anyone could afford, and which had the added advantage of staying curly in the rain. Even sailors on long sea voyages wore wigs, generally of wool, which held a curl even better than horsehair. The wigmakers imported great quantities of human hair—blond hair from the convents of the Netherlands, dark hair from Italy and the Orient. In his *Encyclopédie*, Diderot claimed that the best hair for wigs came from beer-drinking countries like Flanders, venturing that the grain-based brew somehow nourished the strands.

So much hair was imported that Jean-Baptiste Colbert, Louis XIV's brilliant minister of finances, became concerned about all the money leaving the country and tried to stop the imports. But the wigmakers proved that they were able to reverse the deficit by exporting French wigs abroad. Their profession received an additional boost in 1672. Louis XIV, who was proud of his fine natural head of hair, finally began wearing a

When Louis XIV began to wear a wig in 1672, the fashion spread throughout Europe. Henceforth a gentleman seen in public without a wig risked ridicule or disgrace.

wig—an impressive black, leonine creation. In keeping with the grandeur of the clothing, men's wigs, known as "periwigs," were massive—tall on top, bulky at the sides, with mounds of locks tumbling down over the shoulders. Such wigs made it necessary for men to carry mirrors and combs, which they used frequently in public. Although wires were not used to extend the hair, the wigs were bigger overall than any that women wore.

Forty full-time wigmakers were in residence at Versailles. On any given day, hundreds of wigs were dressed with pomade, curled around hot irons, baked in ovens to heat-seal the style, and finally powdered. Charles Panati explains, "Wig fashion at the seventeenth-century French court necessitated that a person's real hair be either clipped short or pinned tightly to the head. Thus 'bobbed', it facilitated slipping on a wig as well as maintaining a groomed appearance once the wig was removed. Both large straight pins and U-shaped hairpins were called 'bobbing pins.'"[8]

A wig was undoubtedly the safest bet for anyone considering a change of hair color. Sources like the *Ladie's Dictionary* of 1694 provided formulas for dyeing hair, but especially if one sought to lighten it, the prescribed ingredients were often horrific and the results far from assured. Recipes for darkening the hair involved natural ingredients; a mixture of elderberries and wine was said to turn the hair black after one application. A vegetable dye, in which radish extract was the primary ingredient, helped to achieve an auburn shade.

In contrast, recipes for blonding, which involved stripping out the hair's pigment, were more of a gamble. The process had not evolved much since ancient times when people smeared their heads with alkaline pastes and sat in the sun to lighten the hair.

Blonding concoctions often included ceruse, a lead derivative. A quart of lye or a pound of lime was mixed with ceruse and warm water,

with saffron or turmeric sometimes added to achieve a yellow tone. This noxious mix was left on the hair overnight and allowed to dry into a hard shell. The next day it was chipped off, at which point it seems miraculous that any hair should be left on the head!

In addition to using these lethal brews, women attacked gray hair with lead combs that darkened each strand with a coating of lead particles. Indulging in this practice for even a brief time meant inhaling the tiny clouds of lead that did not settle on the scalp. It is chilling to imagine the ladies of the court watching Marc Antoine Charpentier's tragic opera *Medée* which was first performed at Versailles in 1693. In it Medea murders her rival Creusa by her offering her a poisoned robe; meanwhile, many of the women were unwittingly shrouding themselves in a toxic veil of their own.

Could it be that two thousand years of lead as a cosmetic was affecting their collective sanity?

And it did not stop at one poison. Elegant noble-women took pinches of arsenic, too, to stay fashionably pale. (Under the poison's influence the blood transports fewer red hemoglobin cells.) By the eighteenth century, Arsenic Complexion Wafers were available to maintain that treasured pallor.[9]

The enormousness of men's periwigs together with the rage for swept-up styles ushered in the first wave of taller coiffures for women. These *tours*, or *commodes*, invited many jokes about how incommodious they were. Erected from hairpieces and pads mixed in with a woman's own hair, they reigned from the late 1680s until 1710, at times reaching two feet tall, which sounds unreasonable until compared with the three-foot headdresses of the 1770s.

Elizabeth Charlotte, the duchess of Orléans and sister-in-law of Louis XIV, wrote in a letter of 1688, "The King told us at table today about a hairdresser called Allart, who dressed the ladies' heads so high in England, that they could not get

Feathers, gauze, ribbons, pearls,

into their sedan chairs, so they have had to have their chairs made higher in order to permit them to follow the French fashion."[10] Louis may have been amused by the story, but he and his courtiers grew to resent these lofty styles. The men, even in their high heels, looked puny alongside. The king continued his objections until 1691, winning a concession when the configuration was cut back to two tiers. The style's height did not actually diminish; rather it tapered like a spire. By 1693, three and four tiers were back again, and the king's complaints had no real impact. On the subject of coiffures, the great warrior, His Royal Highness the Sun King, was no match for his court ladies.

For a short time it was the fashion for the spire to tilt forward, but accidents involving candles put an end to that. Elizabeth Charlotte herself had fallen victim, as Diana de Marly reports: "The Dowager Madame, after a hard day's hunting, fell asleep at her writing table and her *commode*

caught fire from the candles on the table as her head nodded forward. She awoke to find burning sparks raining down on her scalp and eyebrows, but her yells soon brought her ladies to her aid."[11]

Near the end of Louis XIV's reign, the *tours* came tumbling down, due not to any of his edicts, but to his admiration of the countess of Shrewsbury. The wife of the English ambassador, she was presented at Versailles with unrouged cheeks and a small, unpowdered coiffure. When the fashion changed overnight, the bemused king said, "I swear, it irks me to think, with all my authority as King, that when I railed against these coiffures being too high, no one had the slightest inclination to comply with my wishes. Along comes this stranger, a little English nobody, with a low coiffure: suddenly, all the princesses go from one extreme to the other!"[12]

Some of the French ridiculed the countess for her lack of sophistication, but her taste was prescient. The opulence of Louis XIV's court had be-

artificial flowers above and horsehair pads below helped raise silhouettes by up to two feet.

come absurd. A dress made for Elizabeth Charlotte was embroidered with so much gold she could not stand up in it. At his last ceremonial appearance in 1715, the king himself staggered to the throne under the weight of his coat, which had been embroidered with gold and the finest diamonds he possessed.[13] After he died, the heavy ornamentation gave way to the more freely moving *robe volante* and women's dresses with the sparer elegance so evocatively rendered in the paintings of Antoine Watteau. His enchanting scenes typically include a young woman facing away from the viewer, her dress a shimmer of softly-gathered silk, her hair up in a discreet bun or chignon, subtly accented with a ribbon or bow.

At the Viennese court in 1716, however, the fashions set in Louis XIV's heyday were obviously still *de rigueur*. Lady Mary Wortley Montagu describes the Viennese fashion as "more monstrous and contrary to all common sense and reason that 'tis possible for you to imagine."[14]

The hairdressing techniques she mentions were also behind the times: "They build certain fabrics of gauze on their heads, about a yard high, consisting of three or four storeys fortified with numberless yards of heavy riband. The foundation of this structure is a thing they call a *bourlé* which is exactly of the same shape and kind, but about four times as big, as those rolls our prudent milk maids use to fix their pails upon. This machine they cover with their own hair, which they mix with a great deal of false. . . . Their hair is prodigiously powdered to conceal the mixture, and set out with three or four rows of bodkins, wonderfully large, that stick two or three inches from the hair, made from diamonds, pearls, red, green, and yellow stones, that it certainly requires as much art and experience to carry the load upright as to dance upon May Day with the garland."[15]

Discreet Coiffures in the Days
of Madame de Pompadour

When Louis XV ascended the throne in 1715, a lighter decorative style, one that came to be called rococo, was blossoming. The legs of furniture began to curve gracefully; pink roses appeared in powdered wigs. By 1720, women began cutting their hair shorter, and all seemed to signal airiness and frivolity. The cultural supremacy of France was more assured than ever. A great deal of the internationalism of the period was simply the diffusion of French *ésprit* all over the globe, and femininity embodied that spirit as never before. As Karl Toth has written of women in rococo France, "Architecture and furniture design forsake Baroque's spacious solemnity, and snuggle more and more intimately round woman's dainty little person; and in the butterfly world of *la mode* this elusive creature, woman, shaped her whole century unrestrictedly to her own image."[16]

It makes perfect sense that in this period the dominant persona at the French court was a woman. Madame de Pompadour not only led and personified fashion, it was she who made Versailles shimmer as the pinnacle of civilized pleasure and refinement. She first charmed Louis XV at a ball in 1745 and remained his mistress and confidante until her death in 1764. Madame de Pompadour captivated the king for an unusually long time, especially considering her self-assessment as a physically cold person. Her hold on him went beyond the sexual; she kept him in her thrall by offering a steady stream of diversions—new plays, operas, houses, alterations, and decorations. She was a master of transformation and novelty, always upping the ante in a context where the pace of stylesetting was already frantic.

Every aspect of her dress and comportment set fashion, including, naturally, her coiffure. It was petite and ever-charming in its variations, as one of her admirers at court wrote, "A hundred

*The short and delicately
curled coiffure brought into fashion
by Madame de Pompadour
was embellished only by a light
dusting of powder
and a few artificial flowers.*

entrancing ways did she arrange her hair—now powdered, now in all its own silken glory, now brushed straight back, ears showing, now in curls on her neck—till the court nearly went mad attempting to imitate her inimitable coiffures."[17] Most portraits represent her with a small, subtly accented coiffure, but a style she wore around 1745 became her namesake and the term survives even today. Hair worn high on the forehead—either brushed over a pad or "frizzed" (as back-combing was called in the eighteenth century)—became known as a "pompadour."

The hairstyles of the early eighteenth century embodied delicacy and discretion. They were curled close to the head or pulled back into a bun. One finds such accents as a small spray of flowers, or, at most, a jewel or two, *tremblant* on a wire. Caps in linen and lace sometimes covered the pulled-back styles. The placement of a few flowers or a feather was called a *pompon*, and through the 1740s, it manifested the ideal of simple, refined

Samuel H. Grimm,
The French Lady in London.

taste. Newly shorn hair provided wigmakers with the means to create short, tightly curled wigs, in a style called *tête de mouton*, or sheep's head.

Mens' wigs had become lighter as well. Periwigs, now less top-heavy, were worn only by academicians and certain members of the legal profession. The hairpieces worn by everyone else took their cue from the campaign wigs sported by military officers during their tours of duty. These wigs had a large curl or a single braid at the back, tied with a black silk ribbon or held in a small bag.

By the 1760s, however, understated elegance succumbed to a more excessive impulse, and hairstyles began climbing skyward again. In 1763 the new fashion for "Frenched" hair hit London, employing, the wits noted, sufficient wool and padding to stuff a chair bottom. The style caught on despite the fact that that it was immediately caricatured in the press, and that boys in the street threw mud at women wearing the tall headdresses. A Dublin hairdresser in 1768 advertised

If women slept propped up on pillows, elaborate styles could survive for weeks, but hair pomades made of animal fat attracted vermin.

his skills in "stuccowing," noting that while the headdress required one hour for construction and two hours for baking, it would last during the whole session of parliament.[18] The term "stuccowing" was apt, for any curls gracing the headdress were not light, fluffy embellishments, but rock-hard side rolls formed by manipulating the lard-encrusted hair.

Once these costly, time-consuming productions were in place, they were not disturbed for weeks, at which point their stench was surely as noteworthy as their size. A newspaper ode from 1768 asked,

> *When he scents the mingled stream*
> *Which your plastered heads are rich in,*
> *Lard and meal, and clouted cream,*
> *Can he love a walking kitchen?*[19]

Even worse than the odor were the vermin that bred within the plaster. In the same year *London Magazine* published a letter describing what the writer had witnessed when his elderly aunt's hair had been "opened up." He saw swarms of "animalculas," but the coiffeur assured him they could not migrate to other parts of the body, as they were stuck fast in the gluey pomade.[20] No wonder every fashionable lady was armed with a long-handled head scratcher! Earlier, men and women had sought relief from lice by shaving their heads and wearing a wig. But a towering edifice on the head required a good bit of one's own hair as an anchor.

Other sacrifices made for beauty's sake: sleeping in uncomfortable positions and fighting off not only bugs, but the occasional mouse. People who know little else of eighteenth-century hairdressing have probably heard the stories about rodents making their nests in a stylish tower of wool and powder-paste. Needless to say this was a supreme nuisance, but at least it enlivened Sunday church service, as Eleanor Farjeon recounts:

"It cost so much to dress these silly contraptions that the sillier ladies wore them day and night, and sat upright in bed wearing night caps of silver wire to keep out the rats, and a mousetrap on their pillows; for wool and paste attracted mice like larder. But in spite of all precautions, a mouse sometimes slipped inside a wig while a lady dozed, and made its nest there. And it is told of one little girl that she sat in her pew on Sunday and watched with delight the little mouse popping in and out of the tower of hair in the next pew, and quite forgot to attend the parson's sermon on vanity."[21]

These were glory days for hairdressers; by 1767 at least 1200 of them were working in Paris. They called on women at home, making themselves indispensable not only as arrangers of hair, but as social conduits. In the age where gossip usually traveled by letter, the hairdresser passed along the latest in scandals, feuds, and romances immediately—no wonder his visit was so eagerly awaited! Hairdressers were already beginning to style under their first names only. It is not clear how this practice began, but it indicates how thoroughly they had infiltrated the sphere of women. A few had reached "star" status, and it was a coup for a lady to be able to gush familiarly about her dear Philippe or Antoine, especially if he was the current favorite. The coiffeur played an essential role in one of the most important aspects of eighteenth-century socializing, the lingering toilette. The morning ritual of dressing and hairsetting was a multi-tiered affair in which a noblewoman regularly received visitors and friends; it was a relaxed and welcome respite from the otherwise stifling formality of the court.

The hairdresser's tools of the trade were as specialized as those of the surgeon. They comprised, at minimum: a comb set, usually of bone or tortoiseshell; powder in gray, yellow, or the color of the moment; a powdering carrot (a small cartridge for touch-ups) or a swansdown puff; a knife

*The Parisian barber-wigmaker
with his accoutrements, 1697.*

for removing encrusted powder; pads stuffed with
horsehair; a curling iron; dressing or bobbing pins;
a variety of hairpieces (topknots, tresses, plaits);
and a wide assortment of ribbons, laces, pins, and
ornaments.[22] And, of course, the "gooey" element
that made all the artistry possible—bear's grease,
lard, or a scented pomade (sometimes called
pomatum) either in a jar or in stick form. Here is
one hairdresser's recipe for beef pomatum: "Take
some beef marrow, and remove all the bits of skin
and bone, put it in a pot with some hazelnut oil,
and stir well with the end of a rolling pin, adding
more oil from time to time until it is thoroughly
liquefied, and add a little essence of lemon. This
pomatum will keep three or four months and one
uses it like ordinary pomatum."[23]

In matters of hygiene, this most refined age
was shockingly negligent. Most people considered
frequent bathing unhealthy. Even a king's morning regimen, in terms of washing, was little more
than rubbing his face and hands with a bit of

Wigs were alternatively pomaded and powdered to achieve the best set for curls. The powder fell off during the course of the day so that the process had to be repeated every morning. Carle Vernet, The Toilette of the State Prosecutor's Clerc, *c. 1768.*

almond oil and slapping on a generous dose of perfume. A 1770 London publication, *A Treatise on the Hair or Every Lady her own Hair-Dresser*, by Peter Gilchrist, reveals contemporary hairdressing practices. He offers a special aside for readers who bathed, clearly believing the practice to be uncommon: "Those who bathe should never wet their hair, unless it be requisite on account of their health; and if they do, must be careful that it is quite dry before it is curled: for if it be the least wet, the heat of the irons will scorch and deprive it of its substance."[24]

The common practice was to comb hair out rather than wash it. Gilchrist recommends this method for cleansing a child's hair: "The best method of cleaning the head is to dip a linen cloth in a little soft pomatum, or hog's lard and sweet oil beat up together; rub it over the child's head, and wipe it off with a piece of dry flannel; then throw a little hair powder over it, which prevents heating, cleans the skin, and nourishes the hair."[25]

A Parisian guide to health and beauty published in 1766 recommends washing the hair every two weeks in a mixture of ashes, linseed, myrrh, cane root, and white wine. The primary purpose of this concoction was not to cleanse the hair, but to encourage it to grow longer.[26]

Doctors were not yet concerned with problems of the hair and scalp. Many haircare ideas were related to superstitions. Gilchrist notes, "Some imagine it proper to cut the hair at certain times of the moon: it may be so, but I never could perceive any difference."[27] Hair loss was a concern and people questioned why hair turned gray. The causes were mysterious, leaving him to speculate that gray hairs "generally denote old age, yet they are frequent at twenty: and the change is often observed to take place after sickness or violent headaches."[28]

Gilchrist was convinced that the contemporary hairdressing practices were beneficial for the hair. He does warn, however, about leaving the

coiffure in place too long: "Upon the whole, it is evident that dressing is of great benefit to the hair; for the pomatum and powder nourish it; frizzing expands, and gives it a larger body; and while it remains in dress it hath rest at the roots, which saves large quantities that would fall off by frequent combing: yet it is very detrimental to let it go long without being refreshed; for the lacquer of the pins and the powder, gathering in lumps, are apt to make it tear off in the combing out. . . . Likewise, perspiration, the moisture of the hair, and its being confined from the air, may occasion effluvia rather disagreeable."[29]

The Height of Hair Follies

The fashionable coiffures of the latter half of the eighteenth century were the most awe-inspiring hair creations ever. They remained stylish for the better part of two decades, peaking in altitude and ornateness in the late 1770s. Even more incredible than their size was how these headdresses were employed: like altarpieces or billboards—saluting an event, expressing admiration for an individual, even touting a miracle cure for ailments. For example, followers of the pseudo-scientist Franz Anton Mesmer, who "cured" all sorts of illness through a combination of hypnotism and magnetism at his clinic on the Place Vendôme, proclaimed their allegiance by wearing "mesmerized" headdresses strewn with magnets and little figurines representing patients he had treated.

During these two centuries, the kings' mistresses tended to be the reigning stylesetters, and it even happened that a queen was avoided or snubbed by the most amusing people at court. Soon after her marriage to Louis XIV poor Marie Thérèse retired to a life of extreme piety, her chief pleasures being her religious faith and her collection of dwarfs. Stanislas, the exiled king of Poland and father of Marie Leczinska, Louis XV's queen, proclaimed that the dullest queens in Europe were

his wife and, especially, his daughter: "When I'm with her I yawn like at Mass."[30] But when Marie Antoinette ascended the throne as Louis XVI's queen in 1774, she was determined to occupy center stage. Not only that, she vowed to lead fashion with a blinding brilliance. Her ambition was not to be a great queen—her immediate predecessors were no role models in that respect—but to be the most fashionable woman in France. And she succeeded.

In his captivating biography of Marie Antoinette, Stefan Zweig points out that the couturière Rose Bertin, a commoner, staged her own revolution eighteen years before the real one by entering the queen's private rooms and having intimate interviews with her. Zweig explains that, "After she had induced Marie Antoinette to accept some costly 'creation', she proceeded to fleece the court and the rest of the nobility. . . . The unrest throughout the country, the dispute with the Parliament of Paris, the war with England, did not agitate this futile court society half so much as the new *puce* which Mademoiselle Bertin had brought into fashion, or some exceptionally audacious cut of the hooped skirt, or an unprecedented shade of silk just turned out at Lyons. Every lady who valued herself felt bound to monkey the exaggerations of the mode, and a husband remarked with a sigh: 'Never before have French women spent so much money simply in order to make themselves ridiculous.'"[31]

The incredible lavishness at court is borne out by Olivier Bernier's description of a dress worn by the duchesse de Choiseul: "It was made of blue satin, garnished with marten fur, embroidered with gold, adorned with diamonds, each diamond shining in the center of a silver star underlined with gold spangles, and with this dress, further enriched by lace sleeves, the duchesse wore her hair curled and powdered in a coiffure over three feet high which displayed a whole garden with a brook (made of mirror), a

After Vigée-Lebrun, Marie Antoinette.

little jeweled clockwork windmill spinning away, flowers, and grass."[32]

No one was more lavish in her spending than Marie Antoinette, who indulged not only with coiffure and dresses, but with precious jewelry, all the while getting herself deeper and deeper into debt. In 1775 her mother, Empress Maria Theresa of Austria, wrote to her from Vienna, suggesting that her hairstyle seemed more appropriate for an actress than for a queen, and pleading for her not to wear what might be considered *outré*: "A good-looking queen, endowed with charm, has no need of such follies. On the contrary, simplicity of attire enhances these advantages, and is more suited to her exalted rank. Since, as Queen, you set the tone, all the world will hasten to follow you even when you stray into wrong paths. But I, who love my little Queen and watch her every footstep, cannot hesitate to warn her of her frivolousness in this matter."[33] The newspapers, gossip, and reports from well-meaning friends all told

Maria Theresa that her daughter paid no attention to her warning, so again she wrote: "They tell me that from the roots on your forehead your hair rises as much as three feet, and is made higher by the superaddition of plumes and ribbons."[34] She begged her daughter to follow fashion, not to exaggerate it. Marie Antoinette responded by assuring her mother that at Versailles, the court was so used to the lofty headdresses that no one gave them a second look.

One of the queen's headdresses, dubbed *à la jardinière*, was composed of an artichoke, a head of cabbage, a carrot, and a bunch of radishes. Upon seeing this array, one of her court ladies cried, "I shall not wear anything else but vegetables. That looks so simple, and is much more natural than flowers."[35] Benjamin Franklin perceived, at least upon his arrival in 1777, that the aristocratic and court circles had somewhat less lofty headdresses than the parvenues and "fashionables" outside Paris. He may have amended his

first impression over his seven-year stay, but initially he observed, "at Nantes there were no heads less than five, and a few were seven, lengths of face above the top of the forehead. . . . Yesterday we dined at the Duke de Rochefoucauld's, where there were three duchesses and a countess, and no head higher than a face and a half."[36]

The hairdresser Léonard, a virtuoso of the puff and pad, was fast becoming the court favorite. Previously the queen's hairdresser was forbidden to attend anyone else, but Marie Antoinette feared that Léonard might lose his touch if he set only her hair, so she allowed him to expand his clientele. He was in such great demand that women of lesser rank had to settle for an appointment a day or two in advance of an event, then slept sitting up with their heads kept erect by a special cushion. Léonard's importance is confirmed in the memoirs of the marquise de la Tour du Pin, who remembered one visit to Versailles: "We regained our apartments very much fatigued, and remained quietly in our rooms, so as not to disarrange our coiffures, especially when we had our hair dressed by Léonard, the most famous of coiffeurs."[37]

Marie Antoinette spent twice as much time having her hair done than the other court ladies. Despite Léonard, she continued to have her hair arranged by her former coiffeur. He was an unoriginal fellow that she had nonetheless grown fond of, so to avoid hurting his feelings, she permitted him to set her hair on a regular basis. As soon as he left, Léonard dismantled his work and began everything again.

At the English court, Madame d'Arblay (née Frances Burney, a lady-in-waiting to Queen Charlotte), showed in her letters that noblewomen were similarly preoccupied with, and hindered by, their coiffures. She wrote in April of 1780, "This morning, being obliged to have my hair dressed early, I am a prisoner, that I may not spoil it by a hat, and therefore I have made use of my

Inconveniences caused by the enormous masses of hair built up on metal armatures gave rise to countless caricatures. Spectators at the theater complained that they could no longer see the stage and even petitioned the director of the Paris Opera to refuse orchestra seats to any woman whose wig was too high.

M. Darly, The Optic Curls
or the Obligeing Head Dress, *1777*.

captivity in writing to my dear Susy."[38] She describes her toilette as "that eternal business—never ending, never profiting."[39] Her hairdressing session often began at six in the morning and lasted more than two hours, during which time she prayed that her coiffure would be completed before the queen's so that she could fly to her side as soon as she was summoned.

In 1778, when she was twenty-eight years old, Burney anonymously published *Evelina, or The History of a Young Lady's Entrance into the World*, a tremendously popular novel of manners that presented a feminine viewpoint of eighteenth-century society.

Evelina, a young, country-raised beauty, gets her first headdress proper for London society and writes to her guardian: "I have just had my hair dressed. You can't think how oddly my head feels; full of powder and black pins, and a great cushion on top of it. . . . When I shall be able to make use of a comb for myself I cannot tell, for my

hair is so much entangled, frizzled they call it, that I fear it will be very difficult."[40]

The eternal business of a woman's toilette was bothersome, but a matter of great importance nonetheless. This was a high-born woman's equivalent of business hours, when marriages were arranged along with most other aspects of their personal lives. Despite its strict confines, fashion remained perhaps the foremost arena in which a woman asserted her creativity and individuality. Ladies sat at their dressing tables for hours, pondering improvements. Setting a new vogue was a great coup, something that could bring a woman praise and notoriety, making her, if only briefly, the talk of the town.

Through her hairstyle a woman expressed wit or rebellion. The marquise de la Tour du Pin was displeased by the invitation to a ball which specified that women were to be dressed in white (*Les dames seront en blanc*). She deemed this directive "too cavalier" and protested boldly, thus: "I ordered a charming robe of blue crepe, trimmed with flowers of the same color. My gloves and my fan were also adorned with blue ribbons. In my coiffure, arranged by Léonard, were blue feathers. This piece of childish folly had a great success."[41]

Maintaining the Stylish Coif

Elaborate costumes limited the French *courtières'* mobility. They learned to slide, not step, in tiny, high-heeled slippers; it was the only gait possible when the room was crowded with women trailing trains. Even though many doorways were now being constructed with more clearance, it was surely common to see an elegantly dressed lady ruin her entrance by ramming her headdress into the door jamb. On occasion, however, these hairstyles had their advantages. So full and tall was the hair of a certain Englishwoman, Mrs. Fay, that when her coach was attacked by robbers, she was

able to hide both her and her husband's jeweled watches in the recesses of her ample wig.[42]

The following coiffure described by the baroness d'Oberkirch was, she admitted, *génante*, or a nuisance, but it was the latest fashion:

"This blessed 6th of June [my maid] awakened me at the earliest dawn. I was to get my hair dressed, and make a grand toilette, in order to go to Versailles. . . . These Court toilettes are never-ending, and the road from Paris to Versailles very fatiguing, especially where one is in continual fear of rumpling her petticoats and flounces.

I tried that day, for the first time, a new fashion—one, too, which was not a little *génante*, I wore in my hair little flat bottles shaped to the curvature of my head; into these a little water was poured, for the purpose of preserving the freshness of natural flowers worn in the hair, and of which the stems were immersed in the liquid. This did not always succeed, but when it did, the effect was charming. Nothing could be more lovely than the floral wreath crowning the snowy pyramid of powdered hair!"[43]

Hair powdering peaked in Marie Antoinette's day—blue, pink, violet, and yellow each had its moment of vogue. Powder was made from wheat starch, dried and ground. It varied in price according to its fineness and how it was scented and tinted. Powdering was done in powdering closets. There, the powder was blown on with a bellows while a protective cap was worn and the face was shielded by a conical mask. At least that is how most people did it, but there were more eccentric cases, such as the Prince Kaunitz, chancellor of the Habsburg Empire, who would line up twenty bellows-bearing valets, ten on each side, and then dash though the cloud of perfumed powder![44] Great quantities of the stuff were consumed in England as well as in France, so much that a hair-powder tax passed in 1786 soon raised a quarter of a million pounds per year. In various countries, critics pointed to the scandalous waste of the

wealthy wearing flour and wheat starch on their heads while all around them others starved.

By the 1770s, high headdresses could be found in most of the courts and fashionable cities of Europe. Returning from her residence in Constantinople, Lady Montagu admired a Venetian salon with teakwood wigstands fashioned like the arm of a blackamoor: "The wig room at Teatro Fenici is like a magpie's cage. Chatter, innuendo, and riposte. Powder flies, and one's coiffure is dusted with iridescent sequins, a lovely conceit."[45] Women often embellished their arrangements with regional flourishes, sometimes disconcerting. A visitor traveling through Spain in 1773 found that in Cadiz, elegant ladies dressing for the evening "fixed glow worms by threads to their hair, which had a luminous and pleasing effect."[46]

Gentlemen's wigs were also becoming bigger again, enough so that wearers adopted the *chapeau bras*, a hat that was meant to be carried, not worn. Italy was an important stop for young European gentlemen making the Grand Tour, and around 1770, a group who had spent some time there introduced the "Macaroni style" to Paris and London. The look involved an exaggerated toupee built up on wire frames and padded with wool cushions, just like the hairpieces women were wearing. Satirical engravings of the Macaronis were published widely, caricaturing their vanity and their penchant for feminine adornment. (Apart from the Italian origin of the style, the term Macaroni also alluded to homosexuals, who were said to have "Italian tastes.")

Trendiness magnified the importance of all sorts of trivial matters. There were the right places to be seen, modish things to eat, trendy pets to own, "fashionable" times to cry. With headdresses, it was not enough merely to have spent hours on some lavish creation; in order to be truly the height of fashion, it had to be a headdress *de circonstance.*[47] When the French inventors Joseph and Étienne Montgolfier made one of their ascents

The Macaroni Club was founded in London in 1772 by a group of wealthy young dandies who had travelled in Italy and returned with some outrageous ideas about fashion. Their powdered wigs, which towered eighteen inches over their foreheads, were built up of horsehair and wool.

in a hot-air balloon before the court at Versailles in 1783, it was commemorated by a coiffure *à la Montgolfier*, complete with an anchored balloon. All sorts of unlikely events inspired coiffures: after the successful vaccination of the Dauphin against smallpox in 1774, *poufs d'inoculations* showed up in the latest headdresses.

A coiffure worn by the duchesse de Chartres, named *le pouf au sentiment*, was not really a headdress *de circonstance*, but more of a personalized pouf. Her hairstyle epitomized the trend for sentimental panoramas representing people or places for which the wearer had great affection. In her hair one found "at the back, a woman sitting in an armchair holding a baby (an allusion to the newborn Dauphin), on the right, a parrot pecking at a cherry, and on the left, a little black doll (these referred to her pet bird and a servant); this landscape was enveloped in locks of hair snipped from almost every one of the duchesse's relatives: her husband, her father, her father in law, etc."[48]

Meanwhile, Madame de Lauzun featured on her head "ducks swimming in a stormy sea, scenes of hunting and shooting, a mill with a miller's wife flirting with a priest, and the miller leading an ass by its halter."[49] When headdresses were at their tallest, women protected them with large hoods built on collapsible cane arches. Headdresses flattened somewhat in the 1780s, but became wider, which brought on the fashion for enormous hats.

After French victories over the English fleet in 1778, coiffures with maritime themes cropped up at chic *soirées*. A few weeks before the storming of the Bastille, Marie Antoinette blithely appeared at a party in the Hall of Mirrors at Versailles with a replica of the French man-of-war *La Belle Poule* set into her powdered waves. Little did she know how untimely it was to have Léonard carry out such a witty arrangement— engravings of the queen with a tall ship in her hair were widely distributed to illustrate the preposterous extravagance of the ruling class.

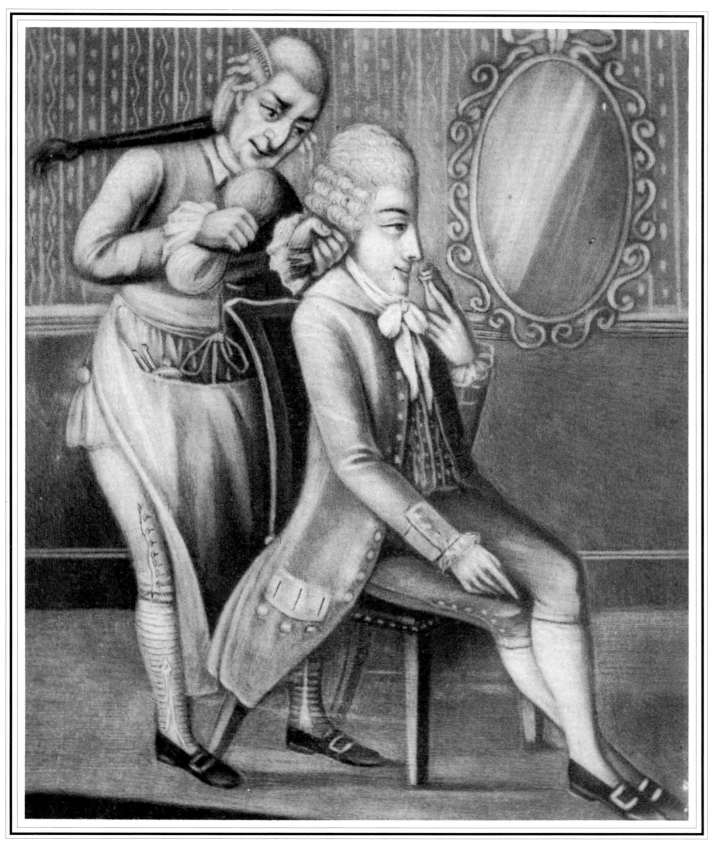

The Lilly-White Maccaroni.

The hairstyle called
"la Frégate la Junon."

The American Revolution,
and a naval skirmish between France
and England in 1778, inspired
a whole range of allegorical coiffures among
the coquettes of the French court.

Revolutionary Changes

In France in 1789, the firestorm of the Revolution descended upon an unwary aristocracy. It had not occurred to the nobles that all their political factionalizing—pamphlets published against Marie Antoinette and various groups, all the examples of waste, corruption, and incompetence they publicized—would bring the downfall of their society as a whole.

The queen was now vilified, with accusations of perversion and treachery maligning her on a daily basis. Not only were people questioning her expeditures, previously unthinkable, but they were protesting the concept of royalty's rule. Revolutionary newspapers and pamphlets were whipping up a frenzy of anti-royalist sentiment, and it was impossible to turn back the tide.

By the time the royal family was imprisoned in the Temple fortress in August 1792, Marie Antoinette's own ash blond tresses had turned completely gray. She was 36 years old. On 19 August, the order was given for the royal family to be isolated. That meant that Marie Antoinette would be separated from her loyal friend, the princesse de Lamballe, who had escaped to London, but returned to stay with her queen to comfort her in those perilous days. As a last token of affection, the queen gave her friend a ring containing a lock of her hair that bore the inscription, "A tress whitened by misfortune."[50] A few weeks later, a revolutionary mob attempted to force their way into Marie Antoinette's prison quarters, bearing the princess's corpse. Just over a year later, a tragic, harrowing year in which two escape attempts went awry, Marie Antoinette was guillotined on 16 October, 1793.

The Revolution had profound repercussions on many aspects of living, including fashion. The elaborate headdresses which now symbolized the decadence of the aristocracy were swept away with the political tide. Hair powdering was

The hairstyle "à la Belle Poule."

For more than fifteen years, Marie Antoinette's extravagant hairstyles were created by the great Léonard Autier, "academician of fashions and coiffures." At his most artistic, he was able to incorporate up to forty-eight feet of cloth or ribbon into a single coiffure.

decried as depriving the new citizenry of bread, an idea that had been raised before. This time, though, the charge was taken seriously, especially during the Reign of Terror, when nobles were put to death for such wasteful measures as burning too many candles. Although the massively scaled coiffures disappeared, the symbolic importance of hairstyles endured, only now they signaled acts of defiance and political sympathies. Poufs *au sentiment* were replaced by *tricolore* bonnets *à la Bastille*. During the Terror, a noble woman's hair was cut short on the neck before she was led to the block.

After the worst of the danger had passed, noblewomen wore red ribbons around their necks as a reminder of the blade they had narrowly escaped, and adopted the closely-cropped coiffure *à la victime* in tribute to friends or relatives who perished on the guillotine. As the century drew to a close, throughout the atrocities of the Terror, hairstyles were short and unpowdered, an

homage to the egalitarian ideals of ancient Rome. Short hair, along with white muslin dresses from England and the West Indies, exemplified the "antique" chic and soon spread across the continent. Despite the toppling of the social order, France still managed to dictate fashion in the courts and capitals of Europe.

Today, one can scarcely believe that the headdresses that towered over the eighteenth century ever existed. A few rare, unpowdered wigs are preserved in museum collections, sometimes in a lovely lacquered wig box, but in general, once a wig was used as part of an ornate, witty hair masterpiece it was discarded.

Evocations of these imaginative coiffures have been passed down to us in letters, memoirs, and portraits—traces of the caprice and frivolity that reigned in the Age of Reason. The hair follies of the late eighteenth century brought new meaning to the phrase "the height of fashion," a height, for better or worse, never to be seen again.

Portrait of the French revolutionary Mirabeau.

Croisat's celebrated "Mode 1830" counterbalanced the leg-of-mutton sleeves and wasp-waist of the contemporary female fashion silhouette—and was a boon to hairdressers.

Tousled Tresses and Corkscrew Curls

decade before the French Revolution, it was impossible for a woman to have too much hair. By the 1790s, she could hardly have too little. Along with the new social order came a radicalized fashion. Some looks from the early 1790s were remarkably similar to the currents of the early 1990s—a natural, unconstructed stylishness that rejected conspicuous luxury. And in both eras, the most daring fashion followers wore transparent dresses. In reaction to the toilettes that went on for hours, the young *élégantes* of the Directory period barely powdered their faces or combed their hair. Women had their portraits painted as they never would have before—with their hair in slight disarray (indicating that they had styled it themselves) or cut extremely short. The fashionably disheveled head could be found in one form or another up until the 1830s.

Any study of the nineteenth century's most whimsical and bizarre hair creations must linger on the earliest decades, from the audacious post-revolutionary styles to the outlandish "Mode 1830." This complicated style was concocted by one of leading coiffeurs in Paris expressly to out-mode the simple styling that was causing such meager times for hairdressers. Hairstyles continued to mirror women's lives and roles. By mid-century, they increasingly reflected the boundaries and restrictions that women faced at every turn. The contrived, "confectionery" arrangements of the 1830s were supplanted by some of the most

During the Directory period, the Incroyables *and the* Merveilleuses *astonished Parisian society with their unkempt hairstyles, eccentric clothes, and libertine behavior.*

unbecoming coiffures ever—severe looks where the hair was twisted and tightly secured to the head. By the century's end, women were back in corsets and crinolines and had adopted an even more bizarre undergarment, the bustle—all elements which concealed or caricatured the female form. Coiffures expanded into ponderous creations that enslaved women anew in laborious setting and upkeep. In light of the fashions and hairstyles of the nineteenth century, it seems that while the world was advancing toward progress and modernism, women were regressing with each passing decade. It was only at the end of the century that they began to reap a few of the seeds of emancipation.

Post-Revolutionary Audacity

After the Revolution, all the rules—not only about elegance, but manners and propriety as well—were revamped to reflect ideals of freedom and a new egalitarianism. "What a change had taken place during my three years' absence!" exclaimed Count Miot de Melito upon his return to Paris in 1795, after serving military duty in Italy. The count witnessed a chaotic mixing of social classes. "All was confusion, and the *salons* were crowded indifferently with Contractors and Generals, with women of easy virtue and ladies of the ancient nobility, with patriots and returned *émigrés*."[1]

The count observed that "Fashion had resumed her sway, and a passion for the antique regulated her decrees, to the detriment of decency."[2] This passion, dubbed *anticomanie*, had a profound effect on fashion and hairstyles. A dress in the antique mode was typically a straight, high-waisted gown of white muslin, so sheer that undergarments could be seen underneath. Women even dampened these light chemises so they would cling more provocatively. The gossamer bodices left little to the

Fanciful hats made a comeback during the Directory period: a crown-shaped toque with heron feathers.

imagination, as can be seen in portraits of the day.[3] It was acceptable, at least for a Parisienne strolling in the gardens of the Palais Royal, to be seen with bare legs, sandals, bracelets around her ankles, and rings on her toes. This was the most extreme, crowd-stopping look among the capricious, libertine fashions adopted in the Directory period by the city's most daring young women— *les Merveilleuses* or the Marvelous Ones.

Their male counterparts, *les Incroyables* or the Incredibles, were criticized for flaunting the latest whims of fashion as previously only women had done. These dandies favored wire-rimmed spectacles (as artifice), long shaggy hair, and tight jackets with huge lapels and flamboyant cravats. Just like today, when the extreme fashions shown on the runway are worn only by a bold few trendsetters, the transparency in women's fashion and the quirkiest styles for men were rarely seen beyond the urbane center of Paris.

L'Anticomanie and the Rage for Blond Wigs

Post-revolutionary fashion was flippant and carefree, and so was the hair. Taking a cue from the wig-loving Roman empress, stylish Parisiennes sported short, curly wigs *à la Faustine*. These wigs were lightweight, unpowdered, and made in a range of haircolors. Messieurs d'Eze and Marcel, whose history of feminine hairdressing was published in France in 1886, wrote, "Coquettes wore a blond wig in the morning and a black wig in the evening. La Tallien changed them several times in the same day."[4] The legendary beauty Thérèse Tallien had at least thirty wigs. This pales in comparison to Empress Faustina's collection of seven hundred, nonetheless, thirty allowed for plenty of switches among style and color. In Paris, blond wigs were the overwhelming favorites—golden, ash, flaxen, strawberry. Scores of epigrams and satires were inspired by the craze, and an author

Wigs were back in style by 1794, although now they were short and colorful.
Perruque à la Ninon.

The short, classically-inspired "Titus Cut" (right and far right) remained popular from the turn of the 18th century through the 1830s and reflected a freedom hitherto unknown for women, although its opponents criticized its too-masculine look as being against the laws of nature.

named Hennion even published *The Secret History of the Blond Wigs of Paris*. These short wigs were liberating for women, but many men were not as fond of "these charms that are left each night on the vanity."[5]

"In the last days of the Directory, the wig was seriously menaced," note d'Eze and Marcel. "Many women were daring to show their natural hair."[6] The ultimate among the natural looks was the "Titus" cut, an extremely short, "fantastic caprice . . . that has no merit other than being the fashion," stated one fashion journal when the style first appeared in 1798.[7] Today we are so used to seeing women in short hair it is hard to imagine how something as natural as this cut could seem so extreme. Coming only a decade after powdered wigs, it opened the door to the concept of a more natural beauty.

As Napoleon came into power, neoclassical styles became wildly popular. Based on the "republican" styles of antiquity, coiffures were

dubbed *à la Vestale* or *à la Caracalla*. For inspiration, hairdressers consulted Greco-Roman heads in bronzes, frescoes, coins, and medallions. The coiffures were also accented with antique motifs, like long hairpins in the form of a lyre. Josephine wore in her hair cameos that Napoleon had brought her from Italy. Jacques-Louis David's famous portrait of Juliette Récamier, the wife of a prominent banker, perfectly captures the vogue: she is reclining on a daybed in the antique style, barefoot, wearing a white muslin gown. Her hair is a short mass of unruly curls, held back by a simple black headband. In fact, David's work is unfinished because of the way he rendered her coal-black hair. He felt a lighter shade better suited both classical convention and the background of the painting. She was not amused and went to David's student François Gérard for another portrait.[8]

Those curly looks in the classical mode were quite difficult to achieve. Women coated their hair with a fixative called "antique oil." If inclement weather caused the curls to refuse to hold, they resorted to a wig or hairpiece. Maria Josepha, Lady Stanley, wrote to a friend in 1802, "My front hair is always coming out of curl in the damp summer evenings, and as I find everybody sports a false *toupée*, I don't see why I should not have the comfort of one, too. I wish it to be as fashionable and deceiving as possible."[9]

Full wigs had given way to hairpieces, intended to augment a woman's own hair. In the coiffure *à la Chinoise*, the hair was drawn up to the top of the head, then a hairpiece or two, much like ponytails, were added. To conceal where the real hair met the hairpiece, the join was wrapped with false braids or ringlets. Honoré de Balzac describes such a style in a short story set in 1809, when a gentlemen points out to his friend a beautiful stranger standing across the room: "Do you see a young woman with a Chinese hairstyle? There, in the corner, on the left; she has blue

Handcolored engraving from Ackerman's
Repository of the Arts, *c. 1810.*

bellflowers in the ringlets of chestnut hair which fall on each side of her head."[10]

Napoleon made a point of resuscitating the French textiles industry, which had suffered under the vogue for simple fabrics. As emperor, he insisted that women not wear the same dress twice to court functions. He bricked up the fireplaces in some palaces, so that anyone who dared arrive scantily clad would freeze. The high-waisted silhouette remained, but the fabrics were once again richly embroidered. The hairstyles remained simple, making the head look small in relation to the new level of finery. So all sorts of hats became popular, many with wide brims worn far back on the head. It was the beginning of the nineteenth-century love affair with all types of millinery. This ultimately resulted in hundreds of styles, from caps to turbans to bonnets.

The French neoclassical style made rapid headway in various European courts, especially in Russia where it was introduced by the exiled portrait painter Elisabeth Vigée-Lebrun, and in Prussia, where it was recorded that Queen Louise adopted it "with more enthusiasm than discretion."[11] The style also made its way to America. Even though a more conservative and covered-up version prevailed there, it was still considered lewd, corrupt, and threatening to the society and virtues of the young nation.

American women who wished to keep up with Parisian styles referred to fashion plates and periodicals, but also to personal letters which tended to be chock full of news on recent looks. Most Americans did not adopt the extremes, but at least one renowned beauty dared to: Elizabeth Patterson. She was the daughter of a wealthy Baltimore merchant and had married Jerome Bonaparte, Napoleon's younger brother. Her gowns were imported from Paris. After their marriage the couple spent some time in Washington, where she scandalized polite society with her fashionable attire. As one society chronicler noted: "She had

Juliette Récamier as seen by the painter Gérard.

French fashion as well as Johann Winckelmann's writings on Herculaneum and Pompeii inspired the neoclassical look among the elegant women of Germany. C. G. Schick, Frau von Cotta, 1802.

made a great noise here, and mobs of boys crowded round her splendid equipage to see what I hope will not often be seen in this country, an almost naked woman. An elegant and select party was given to her by Mrs. Robt. Smith; her appearance was such that it threw all the company into confusion . . . the window shutters being left open, a crowd assembled round to get a look at this beautiful little creature. . . . Her dress was the thinnest sarcenet and white crepe . . . her back, bosom, and part of her waist and her arms were uncover'd and the rest of her form visible. She was engaged the next evening at Madm P's (Pinchon), Mrs. R. Smith and several other ladies sent her word, if she wished to meet them there, she must promise to have more clothes on."[12]

American women could adopt the French hairstyles without causing such a scandal. Josephine du Pont, a transplanted French woman whose husband worked in the diplomatic corps, reported that her short blond wigs "have become

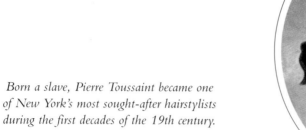

Born a slave, Pierre Toussaint became one of New York's most sought-after hairstylists during the first decades of the 19th century.

the envy of all women, and have made the fortune of a coiffeur, who after ruining a half dozen, managed to copy them rather well. He sells them for twelve dollars. . . . They are light, natural, and charming."[13] While the short wigs caught on quickly, they were not always easy to obtain, as the fashion historian Michele Majer reports, "In December Madame du Pont had to tell her friend: 'Once again, renounce your blond circlet for the present. Thirty times I have sent to the maker, but there is no way to get anything from him. He pretends that the hair he had set aside for us was burned in the oven! What a misfortune! What a calamity for the New York Belles!'"[14]

The Saintly Toussaint

In 1793, an uprising in the French colony of Saint Domingue (now Haiti), sent thousands of émigrés—including hairdressers, jewelers, and other practitioners of the fashion trades—north to America. One was Pierre Toussaint, a black man who would become New York society's most sought-after coiffeur. Born a slave on the Bérard family plantation in 1766, he became a favorite of Mrs. Bérard, was educated and granted access to the family library. As political unrest began to brew on Saint Domingue in 1787, the Berard family took up what they believed to be temporary residence in New York City and Toussaint was apprenticed to a hairdresser.

In *Echoes of a Belle*, a lady writing under a pseudonym provides a glimpse of him at work: "The illustrious Toussaint, with his good tempered face, small earrings, and white teeth, entered the room, his tall figure arrayed in a spotless apron. The curling tongs were heated, and there was a perfume of scorched paper as Toussaint commenced operations. Alice shrank from the sight of her tortured head which, in a hundred 'papillotes' seemed to stand upon end in every direction. The elaborate 'coiffure' was completed,

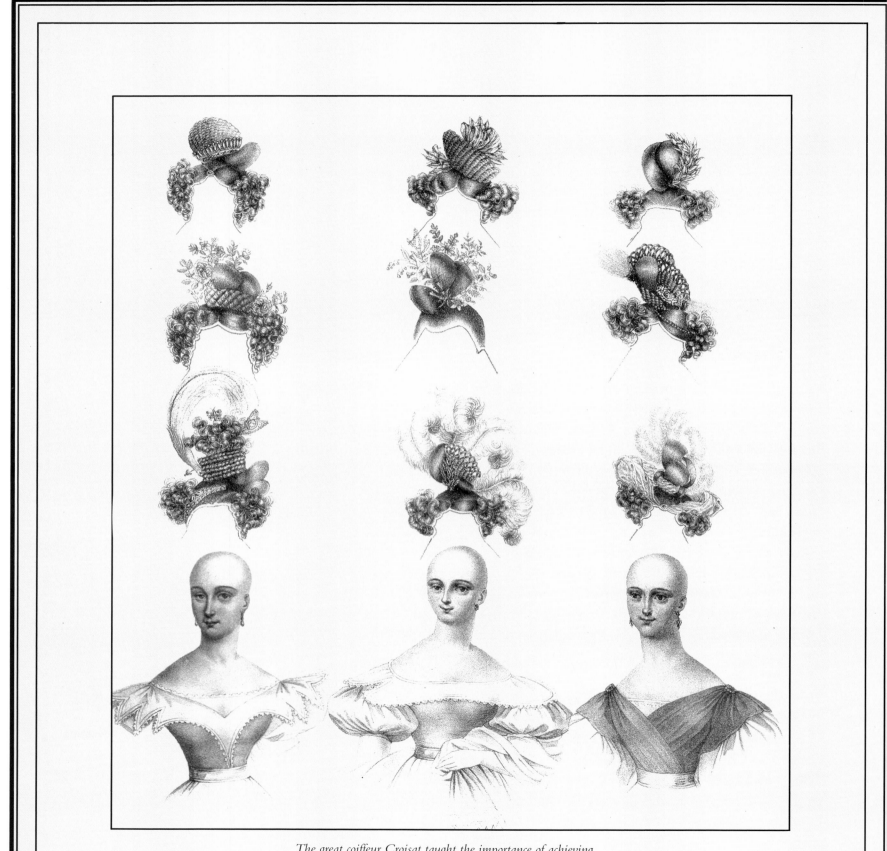

*The great coiffeur Croisat taught the importance of achieving
the effect of upward thrust to counterbalance the sloping shoulders, the deep decolleté and wide skirts
of contemporary fashion. Plates from* Théorie de l'art du Coiffeur, *Paris, c. 1840.*

The Mode 1830.

hairdressers of France and England were all suffering extreme hardship. . . . The prevailing coiffure was a flat, simple dressing, so crude, in fact, that the ladies, or their maids, could dress it without the aid of a professional hairdresser."[18] Heaven forbid! But just when prospects for the profession looked bleakest, a Parisian hairdresser named Croisat stepped into the breach. Croisat, who was known as "hairdressing's Napoleon," perceived his mission to be, in his own words, "to create a genre of coiffure which must be at the same time in good taste, and impossible for amateurs to execute."[19] He accomplished this by creating a vogue for coiffures so ridiculously contrived they sent women back to the professionals. Croisat's famous "Mode 1830" brandished huge topknots of horsehair, wrapped with wreaths, bows, and braids. The hair lay flat against the head in front, then the remainder of the hair was twisted around metal forms. High combs and triple wire-mesh loops gave shape to these cre-

ations, which resembled volcanic eruptions of frou-frou. The tallest arrays required as many as seven combs to hold all the "garnishes" in place—feathers, fur, and jewels mixed in with heavy bunches of pendulous curls. Croisat established a hairdressing academy to teach his techniques and in 1836 published a book, *Les Cent-un Coiffeurs de tous les Pays* (*101 Hairdressers from all Countries*). The nemesis of Croisat and his followers was, of course, the Titus style, the closely-cropped cut that had freed women from elaborate hairdressing. It proved to have remarkable staying power, remaining influential for more than thirty-five years. Attempting to rid the profession of this irritating mode, Croisat embarked upon an anti-Titus campaign. He attacked the style in his book, noting that it gave women "a male air" and that it "deprived them of the beauty particular and distinctive to their sex. . . . You never see Eve, Venus, or the Graces painted with cropped hair."[20] He then delivered the cruelest blow: "Women,

The 1840s brought the return of a more maneagable hairstyle characterized by a central part flanked by curls, braids, or ringlets, which accentuated the oval shape of the face (right and opposite).

Victorian submissive woman, with the full skirts and flat-heeled slippers."[30]

Flat-heeled shoes might seem liberating, but many of the slippers of the period were so flimsy they would often be "danced through" in an evening. The idea was that the woman's place was indoors—protected, and certainly not taller than her husband. A woman was not fully dressed until she was trussed up in a battery of under-skirts and overskirts, chemises and petticoats, drawers and camisoles. Garments that closed with back fasteners and hooks reinforced the condition of dependence: women could hardly dress themselves without the assistance of sisters or maids. How different they appeared from women circa 1800! The dropped waistline had put women back in corsets. And by the 1850s, the balloon-shaped crinoline put them, literally, in a cage. In France, Empress Eugénie was called *la reine crinoline*, making this cumbersome contraption obligatory for fashionable women during the Second Empire.

Not only was it awkward, it was downright dangerous: the trellis-like construction made it quite easy to catch one's foot and fall down stairs.

If the hairstyles that endured over several decades—a central parting flanked by curls, ringlets, or waves—had an appeal in their own era, it was an eroticism borne out of repression. The fashion historian C. Willett Cunnington observed, "Sometimes a single curl will lie pendant on a white shoulder, a veritable serpent near forbidden fruit . . . Victorian ringlets converted the face into a delicate oval, harmonizing with the fragile consumptive charm which bewitched gentlemen of that period, when signs of rude health in young ladies were viewed askance."[31]

What brought about these drastic changes in the way women dressed and behaved? One major factor was the rise of the middle class, whose values are often the most conservative in the social spectrum, initiating more rigid standards of propriety. "Perhaps there never was another period in

history when it would be so true to say that the wife was considered theoretically an angel and was practically a slave," Laver wrote.[32] This could be said for women of all classes. Poor women were sold as brides; prostitution and indentured servitude were rampant. Even for upper class women, the eighteenth-century notions of pleasure and privilege were long gone. Now the operative ideas for the feminine sex were sacrifice and filial duty. Sheltered, infantilized, with few outlets for creativity beyond the confines of the home, recreational "handiwork" flourished.

Teapots and Crucifixes of Hair

The ideal Victorian woman was benignly artistic, producing all sorts of knick-knacks and what-nots, which were to be counted among her "achievements." Rita Wellman notes in the book *Victoria Royal*: "She was forced to spend many hours in the house, and in a kind of unconscious revenge

she went to a great deal of trouble to 'beautify' it. Every room had some evidence of her industry and creative urge, some object bound, tied and streaming with hand-painted ribbons, some article of 'utility' which she has fashioned and covered with forget-me-nots, cupids, blue birds, lilies-of-the-valley, peacocks and hearts."[33] With this mad frenzy of decoration, one realizes why Victorian interiors had a cloying aspect. Women's absolute passion, though, was yet another handicraft: the hair jewelry they painstakingly wove by following pattern books. Beginners practiced with horsehair, which was thicker and easier to manipulate. As their facility grew, they used their own hair or bought hair, which was then boiled and sorted. They sat in the parlor and made everything from earrings to crucifixes, maybe even a fob chain for the watch of their fiancés. Today, these strange relics are usually framed or preserved under glass.

Just how did women create these densely-woven baubles? They used a braiding table with a

The advent of the bustle and the vertically pleated skirt brought a taller and narrower hair silhouette. Greater volume in back was achieved by an impressive array of hairpieces with cascading ringlets.

hole in the center; bobbins wound with lengths of hair hung down around the edges. Consulting dizzyingly complex diagrams, they crossed the bobbins under and over one another until they had a chain of braided hair that dropped though the center hole, pulled taut by a lead weight. There were taller tables for men who braided, although the texts suggest that it was primarily women who engaged this activity: "Of the various employments for the fingers lately introduced among our countrywomen, none is more interesting than hair work. . . . This work has now become a drawing-room occupation, as elegant and free from all the annoyances and objections of litter, dirt, or unpleasant smells, as the much-practiced knitting, netting, and crocheting."[34]

Ropes and chains woven from hair were taken to the neighborhood jeweler who finished these treasures with gold or brass fittings, sometimes even a hidden compartment for daguerreotypes. In a short story by Balzac, a young Parisian

is touched to receive a gift from the woman he loves—a set of handkerchiefs embroidered with her hair, which he assumes she herself had created especially for him. He is dismayed to walk into a shop and learn that such gifts are the latest fashion, and that the intricate hair sewing is in fact the handiwork of the shopkeeper's wife.[35]

The Crystal Palace exhibition held in London in 1851 was, as Wellman writes, "England's pride and the envy of the whole world." She describes it as filled with "grotesque oddities, outmoded to the point of absurdity, slightly repulsive creations, particularly where the decorative and applied arts were concerned."[36] Among the English craftwork was an astonishing curiosity—a tea service made entirely from hair![37] Whether the pieces were inset with ceramic, i.e. meant to be used, or whether they were merely a *tour de force* of hair weaving doesn't matter—the idea that someone bothered to create an entire tea service from hair achieves an unexpected combination of incompat-

The fashion for hairpieces made for an important international commerce in hair: two hundred thousand pounds of it was imported into the United States between 1859 and 1860.

ibles provoking a sense of revulsion that even the Surrealists would have envied.

With so much of women's lives centered in the home, hairdressers began to offer maintenance products along with simple hair attachments for self-styling. By 1865, fashion plates show a range of beautifully designed hairpieces: braids, curls, and buns which a woman could simply clip on. A new crop of products was introduced to maintain the natural beauty of the hair and to tint graying locks. One might think that these hair "renewers" might finally be made with more sensible ingredients. On the contrary, in his study of the diseases of the hair and scalp, Dr. Benjamin Godfrey found that products like Rossetter's Hair Restorer and Hall's Vegetable Sicilian Hair Renewer were commonly laced with lead compounds at least a century after the dangers of lead were acknowledged.[38]

By the 1870s, women's lifestyles were becoming less sheltered and they were beginning to incorporate activities outside the home. The advent of the beauty salon was imminent. Newly built department stores offered hairstyling salons, and it had become acceptable for a woman to visit a beauty parlor, rather than having the hairdresser come to her. Martha Harper opened her first shop in Rochester, New York. She eventually developed a chain of five hundred locations—the first salon franchise—a notable achievement considering that men still held the monopoly in both the business and creative sides of the profession.

In America, many were still following Parisian hairstyles. Publications like *Godey's Lady's Book* kept them current on fashion trends. With the Civil War and the push westward, however, women were more concerned with sensible clothing, and a few of them were beginning to call for more emancipated dress.

Amelia Jenks Bloomer proposed the "bifurcated skirts" that became known as "bloomers" in place of the "rigid adherence to feminine fashion adopted at profligate courts in Europe."[39] Mrs.

Belle Johnson, Three Women, *c. 1890.*

Models from a German hairstyling album c. 1890.

hair measuring 8 feet, 3 inches.[45] These were extreme cases, but ordinary women also had very long tresses.

A woman whose long hair was naturally wavy was fortunate indeed. But those Parisiennes endowed with stick-straight hair could turn to Marcel Grateau, who introduced in the 1880s the Marcel wave or "ondulations," a waved effect created by using curlers and heated irons. This innovation made Marcel's fortune; he retired in 1897 with savings of a million francs. Although this process did not involve chemical treatment, it was an important precursor to the permanent wave. It influenced not only the upswept, wavy styles of the Belle Epoque, but also the short finger-waved styles which held fast until the Second World War.

As the population and industrialization expanded in Europe, the aristocracy retreated into its own world, hidden away from the noise and bustle of modern life. The Parisian nobility was completely sealed off from the rest of the city,

which gave it an incredible mystique. In the novels of the late nineteenth century, one reads about ladies of breathtaking elegance who led their lives moving from their gaslit, upholstered interiors to their lavishly appointed carriages.

Marcel Proust, describing an evening at the opera in *The Remembrance of Things Past*, contrasted the hairstyles of two women of the aristocracy. The face of the princess of Guermantes was framed by a fantastic arrangement "At once plume and blossom, like certain subaqueous growths, a great white flower, downy as the wing of a bird, fell from the brow of the Princess along one of her cheeks. . . . Over her hair, reaching in front to her eyebrows and caught back lower down at the level of her throat, was spread a net upon which those little white shells which are gathered on some shore of the South Seas alternated with pearls . . ."[46] Her cousin, the duchess of Guermantes, opted for a more subdued gesture (which he preferred), "The Duchess wore in her hair only a

Vintage postcards c. 1900
often feature demure young women
with ponderous coiffures.

out with pads and garnished with amber, tortoise-shell, or imitation diamond combs. On black Mondays, after a long solitary session with her arms upraised, putting the waves and curls into place, the effect might still not please her.

"Then she would take out the rats, glancing with alarm into the looking glass as the whole business started over again. Her face became flushed, her arms would be aching, and by the time she had finished she was more than late for dinner."[2]

Despite all the hair to care for, there was a limited range of haircare products—nothing like the shampoos, conditioners, and styling aids available today. *The Woman Beautiful*, published in 1901 by Ella Adelia Fletcher, provides various recipes for the hair, most of which sound more like a science experiment than a nourishing treatment. She recommends washing the hair once every two weeks, stating that "there is no better shampoo for the hair than an egg, well-beaten with about an ounce of water, and rubbed thor-

oughly into the scalp."[3] In terms of conditioning, she was a great believer in various pomatums, one of her favorites a concoction of petroleum jelly, castor oil, Gallic acid, and oil of lavender. Her recipes often contained natural herbal oils, which seems reasonable. But most of the shampoos consist of harsher stuff like bay rum, alcohol, or ammonia—ingredients powerful enough to remove petroleum jelly and eliminate the "curd" that formed when the oily runoff met with hard water.

Shampooing a great mass of hair was a relatively simple prospect compared with styling it. Women had only sticky dressings like "bando-lines and mucilaginous fluids" to keep their hair in curl.[4] Fletcher cautions against using a curling iron, which, she correctly asserts, damages the hair's fiber. Instead she suggests applying a gum arabic, bichloride of mercury, and lavender water compound, then setting the hair in the desired arrangement as it dries.[5]

An advertisement for Petrole Hahn hair products shows the coiffeur working with a woman's abundant tresses. Cleansing and styling often involved primitive concoctions, laced with alchohol and other harsh substances.

She cautions against another procedure developed in France by furriers and felt manufacturers. Despite the corrosive effects of the *secretage* method (its main ingredients were quicksilver and nitric acid) women nonetheless used it to wave the hair: "The operation is conducted before a fire, or in a current of warm air, so that the hair may dry as quickly as possible. The moistened hair is loosely adjusted into the desired positions . . . when partly dry, it is 'put up' in greased curl-papers. In a few hours, or sooner, the hair is washed with tepid water (without soap), dried, and slightly oiled. On being now gently combed and brushed, it generally shrinks up into small crisped or wavy locks; and it will generally retain this property for two or three weeks, or even much longer."[6]

The first permanent waving machine, which modified the hair through heat and chemistry, was introduced in 1906 by the inventor Charles Nessler, who later changed his name to Nestle. Some type of alkaline reagent, such as borax or ammonia, was applied to break down the hair's structure. Then the brave client's tresses were wound around rods, tightly tethering her to the waving machine—a frightening contraption with heat-conducive metal curlers dangling on cords suspended from the ceiling. In its earliest days, the perming process was prohibitively expensive (by some accounts costing $1,000), and time consuming, taking up to eight hours.[7] Aside from the time and expense, it ruined quite a few heads of hair when the electric waving rods were set too tight or not tight enough. With long hair, the process was an ordeal. Permanent waving would not catch on in a major way until shorter, more manageable, and easier-to-curl hair became the fashion.

Some women's hair tumbled down to their knees, other's almost to the floor. Drying it could be a trying task. As Charles Panati explains, the time was ripe for the first hair dryer, although it emerged via a strange route: "An early advertisement for the so-called Pneumatic Cleaner illustrated

107

When the "bob" swept Europe and America the art of hairdressing centered for the first time on the quality of the cut rather than on the artifice of style. Louise Brooks prompted thousands of women to follow her example, c. 1928.

Josephine Baker's hair took so beautifully to the sleek, 1920s style that a French hair product company made her its model.

a woman seated at her vanity, drying her hair with a hose connected to the vacuum's exhaust. With a why-waste-hot-air philosophy, the caption assured readers that while the front end of the machine sucked up and safely trapped dirt, the back end generated a 'current of pure, fresh air from the exhaust.'"[8] As soon as a small, low-powered motor was developed for the blender in 1920, the hand-held hair dryer was introduced.

With such bother involved in caring for and styling the hair, one can see why the fashion for short hair in the late 1920s was arguably as liberating as getting the vote. Antoine was to play a major role. A man just slightly ahead of his time, he had the good fortune of seeing the times catch up with him, making him the most celebrated and sought-after hairdresser of the early twentieth century. Within a few years of his arrival in Paris, he had a loyal coterie of women on whom he worked his magic—namely, scaling down the mountainous arrangements and experimenting with waves and sculptured curls that

hugged the head in a stylized, undulating pattern.

Antoine had cut his first "bob" in 1910 to make the actress Eve Lavallière look younger for a role she played at the Comédie Française. Though he was deluged with requests for the cut, he did not feel that the time was right for it. Nevertheless, two years later he succumbed: "About 1912 a bell rang inside my head. The time had come for women to have their hair short. This new automobile in which women sat open to the winds, these new women with careers, this busy life. And these clinging clothes, which demanded small, neat heads, not enormous masses of hair."[9]

In 1913 the ballroom dancer Irene Castle became the first American celebrity to sport the bob. While performing the new, faster ballroom dance numbers with her husband, Vernon, her hairpins occasionally flew out and hit members of the audience! One fateful day she grabbed a pair of scissors and snipped off her hair to just below the ears. The Irene Castle bob made headlines.

To Bob or Not to Bob

Society was becoming more open, even the rarefied province of "high" society. Proust's Paris and Edith Wharton's New York (where ladies put their new purchases from Paris away for a year, so as not to appear too fashionable) were losing ground to the new rules of "cafe society." The First World War had wrought decisive changes, including a swift emancipation for women in the workplace, but it was assumed that after the war, they would resume their pre-war duties and roles. Women working in the ordinance factories cut their hair in great numbers, although not as short as the severe crops to come in the late 1920s. Despite the war and other matters of grave importance, short hair was the subject of volatile debate. Antoine ventured, "In the terrible great war that was tearing nations apart, I believe people found great relief in arguing about a small thing like whether to bob or not to bob."[10]

The urge to escape, even momentarily, from the harsh realities of the war brought on a wave of brightly colored wigs. Sonia Delaunay introduced red and green wigs to accompany the Cubist-inspired clothing she designed for her Paris fashion house.[11] Antoine, too, had many requests: "In black times of despair, women try harder than usual to seem gay and lighthearted. . . . My clients suddenly blossomed out in wigs of strange, bright colours, orange and blue and purple, red and snow white, any colour that had no relation to real hair. Jade green was especially effective. . . . It is a sort of defiance. It says to the enemy, 'You can't beat us. We will win no matter what you do.' One client told me that she put hers on when she was alone because it made her feel like someone else, which was, she said, 'a great relief.'"[12]

Antoine himself had a passion for white satin frock coats and he was not at his best unless he was surrounded by white flowers. He even slept in a glass coffin, claiming that glass enclosures protected him from harmful electric rays in the

Fantasy hairstyles from the 1920s.

atmosphere. Yet for all his eccentricities, he was a great innovator who was obsessed by, and perfectly in tune with, modernity. He perceived the change in the air and launched a fashion that acted upon it. He recognized that along with such influence came a measure of responsibility. "It is exciting to lead fashion, to start vogues, and I have been charged with doing that too often and too boldly. But I have never started anything just because it was new."[13]

In the twenties, his ideas took hold. Drawings published in *Vogue* show the new woman of fashion with chin-length hair, in a drop-waisted Chanel evening gown, applying lipstick in public, one of the new gestures with which young women scandalized their mothers. Josephine Baker hit Paris in 1924 and soon afterward advertisements appeared promoting a product to achieve her sleek style—"*pour se bakerfixer les cheveux.*"[14] Baker had a collection of Antoine's short, sculpted wigs, which she wore like hats.

Bobs: Defiant and Inevitable

With long hair so labor-intensive, one might wonder why women would hesitate to cut it at all. But it was not merely a question of convenience or fashion. Women's lives were bound by convention and cutting one's hair short defied the social order. As the bob, and a shorter, ear-length bob called the "shingle" were taken up around the world in the late 1920s, outrage and debate reverberated in their wake. Suffragettes and women in intellectual circles adopted the bob to symbolize their drive for emancipation. *Photoplay* magazine reported, "Perhaps it is the result of the war, perhaps it is the motion pictures, but all over the country such headlines are common: 'Bobbed hair leads to suit for divorce.' 'Bobbed hair bandit shoots cashier who objects to being robbed.' 'Shocked husband shoots himself when wife bobs her hair.'"[15]

The church opposed bobbed hair and so did the business world. Antoine recalled, "Marshall

London 1932. The latest hairdressing craze for ladies was to have their hair colored to match or contrast artistically with an evening frock. Every color was possible, including mother-of-pearl.

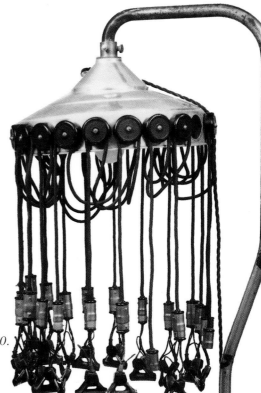

The permanent-waving machine opened a whole new range of style possibilities for women. But the machines were often poorly grounded, providing electric shocks along with the newly-curly hair. c. 1930.

Field in Chicago refused to employ women with bobbed hair. In Paducah, Kentucky, five nurses in training at a hospital school were suspended for cutting their hair. And so on, everywhere. The University of Arkansas demonstrated by tests that long-haired women have the best minds."[16]

Despite all the controversy, the bob's progress was inevitable. In the words of a woman living in London, "All the young women at the office were having their hair cut short . . . my mother and I went to a hairdresser's on Wardour Street, where we sat at the end of a long queue of women who, like us, were patiently waiting to let down their beautiful long hair. An hour later, with hats far too large for our diminished heads, feeling very self-conscious, anxious to be home where we could make a minute, pitiless examination of our changed appearance, we emerged as new women."[17]

Louise Brooks, so beguiling in her shiny black helmet of hair, prompted thousands of women to follow suit. But not every woman's profile took to the bob as beautifully. Douglas Fairbanks summed up the situation when he commented, "I think it is beautiful for some, but sensible for all. Therefore, some women look beautiful with bobbed hair, while others look . . . just sensible."[18]

The catastrophe of an unsuccessful bob is portrayed by F. Scott Fitzgerald in the short story "Bernice Bobs Her Hair." Bernice is cornered into cutting off her beautiful hair by her spiteful cousin: "Twenty minutes later the barber swung her around to face the mirror, and she flinched at the full extent of the damage that had been wrought. Her hair was not curly, and now it lay in lank lifeless locks on both sides of her suddenly pale face. It was ugly as sin—she had known it would be ugly as sin. Her face's chief charm had been its Madonna-like simplicity. Now that was gone and she was—well, frightfully mediocre—not stagy; only ridiculous, like a Greenwich Villager who had left her spectacles at home."[19]

The Shock of Permanent Waving

The need to enhance these newly-cropped heads made a great many women take another look at Nestle's permanent wave. While there were new variations involving steam or hot jets of ammonia, the process was still extremely risky. A technical manual for the trade entitled *The Art and Craft of Hairdressing*, published in the mid-1930s, devotes an entire section to the treatment of burns due to waving, describing some serious enough to merit emergency treatment. Sometimes the porcelain rods overheated and their bakelite covers melted, with some poor woman ending up with a head covered with molten plastic.[20] A more common problem was the customer's receiving electrical shocks. The manual warns, "The continual heating and cooling of these substances [the reagents] some-times produce microscopic cracks though which steam and reagent could percolate, thus once again causing 'shorts' with shocks and even explosions."[21]

*Daisy Fellowes, photographed by Horst in the costume
she wore for her "Bal Oriental" in Paris in 1935.
The sculpted curls of her wig were a trademark of the hairdresser Antoine.*

Many women were put off by the idea of being anchored to, and possibly zapped by, this daunting apparatus. Research continued. By the end of the thirties, a two-step chemical process involving a much milder reagent and a neutralizer was developed—lessening the importance of heat, and therefore, the machine. Finally, the process was reliable enough even for home use.

One major gain was initiated by permanent waving: it brought a great many women into the hairdressing profession. Census reports show that in London at the turn of the century, only one in ten hairdressing professionals was a woman, a figure that included cashiers and other salon assistants.[22] It should come as no surprise, though, that the work newly open to women was of the most laborious and unhealthy sort, involving continuous exposure to chemical fumes.

Another way women embellished their sleek bobs was with a single curl fixed onto their face with setting lotion. The photographer Brassaï wrote

in *The Secret Paris of the 30's*, "The dance hall also had its fashion in dress, and this was the real folk costume of Paris. The girls wore skirts with suspenders, satin blouses, and those spit curls—or kiss-curls—which were so typical: small coiled locks of hair flattened onto the forehead or the temples."[23]

By the thirties, salons had become an integral part of a woman's ritual of beauty. Those who were very much in the public eye might have their hair styled several times a day.[24] Speaking of Daisy Fellowes, Antoine claims, "She does not, like the Duchess of Windsor, have her hair done three times a day. She changes her coiffure ten times a day, and these are real and basic changes, for she is like quicksilver."[25] One suspects that Antoine may have had ulterior motives in advocating this chic, like Croisat did when he promoted the "Mode 1830."

Antoine followed up his acclaimed sculpted look with a new, softer style. American *Vogue* reported in 1928: "A direct reaction from the severe

The Windblown Coiffure, c. 1930.

115

JEAN HARLOW – Metro *Goldwyn* – Mayer

MG-29423
MGM

As Jean Harlow ascended to stardom, women attempted to mimic
her look with homemade peroxide and ammonia pastes.

The countess of Oxford and Asquith, photographed by Cecil Beaton.

The First Platinum Blondes

bobs of recent yesterdays have appeared in the development of what the French call 'floue' in coiffures. Literally, floue means light, fluid, flowing, but in coiffures, it means a tendency toward soft ringlets."[26] *Vogue* called the style "at once so natural and so complex," and it was, of course, a great boon to hairdressers. This look of short waves culminating in a graceful display of curls was very becoming, but by no means easy to set. The hair was dampened with a setting lotion (concocted from gum mucilage, alcohol, and borax), then waved with the hand. At the ends, each lock of hair was arranged in a circle, using at least two pins, thus they were called pin curls. Finally, the hair was dried and carefully combed. Elsa Schiaparelli, the couturier known for her inventive, surrealistic designs, was one of the first to sport the *floue* to great effect. Janet Flanner observes in a 1932 *New Yorker* profile: "Though she is magnificently straight-haired, Antoine has recently launched a mode by puffing up her hair in curls."[27]

Adventurous women persisted in the dream of changing the color of their own hair. In 1909, dyes were first offered commercially. Yet by the 1930s, the formulas still contained chemical levels so toxic that, at times, customers' eyes swelled shut and their foreheads began to blister. Women often left the salon with violent headaches. As Gilbert Foan states in his influential manual, "A number of hairdressers have been involved in legal costs, and in some cases additional heavy damages have been awarded to clients who have become poisoned by a hair dye application. So serious have been some of the cases that many insurance companies now refuse to cover a hairdresser against what is known as 'hair dye risks.'"[28]

In the twenties, a mystery that had endured since ancient times was finally solved—the first double-process blonding was developed. In this procedure, the pigment is stripped out of the hair,

Sydney Guilaroff styled hair for more than 800 films. Among his most inventive accomplishments were the burnished golden curls Marlene Dietrich wore in Kismet, *1944.*

then a toner applied to achieve the desired shade. With this technique, the hair becomes a blank canvas, receptive to any hue. By applying diluted methyl violet or methylene blue, stylists could attain the lightest-possible silvery shade—one that came to be called platinum blond. Hollywood soon realized the potential of this haircolor, which looked so luminous and ethereal on the silver screen. Sultry, dark-haired seductresses like Pola Negri and Clara Bow were eclipsed by the screen goddess Jean Harlow, who even starred in a film entitled *Platinum Blonde* in 1931.

Women everywhere were joining the ranks of the haircoloring pioneers. Janina Trasko, my mother, remembers one popular home remedy. "I would mix Marchand's peroxide with ammonia, then add a few tablespoons of Ivory soap flakes to make a paste. You only needed to leave it on your hair for a few minutes. I don't think I ever read this recipe anywhere. It was one girl telling another. After seeing Jean Harlow at the movies,

we all wanted to be blonde."[29] Films of the 1930s glamorized high society, but it was Hollywood's version, an elegant fantasy world to distract depression-era audiences. The direction was clear: high society defined fashion less, Hollywood defined it more. The studios packaged and publicized actors and actresses until they had an image to which the public responded. When an actress changed her haircolor for a role, hundreds of letters poured in from fans, demanding either that she return to her original color or that she make the change permanent.

Even though he was active before hairdressers became household names, Sydney Guilaroff, Metro-Goldwyn-Meyer's top hairstylist, became one of Hollywood's most important image makers. He contributed to the urbane chic of one of the most stylish films ever made—George Cukor's *The Women.* For the lavishly costumed production *Marie Antoinette,* starring Norma Shearer, he designed two thousand powdery

white wigs, including a birdcage headdress and scores of outrageously feathered and festooned creations. Then there was *Kismet*, an oriental fantasy in which he transformed Marlene Dietrich into a blonde exotic who sported a twisted arrangement of coiled braids set off by tiny ringlets. He also gave her tendrils, molded stiff then coated with gold leaf, like decorative ironwork. Along with the photographer George Hurrell and the costume designer Adrian, Guilaroff created the look of Hollywood's golden age.

Throughout the Second World War, people continued to turn to the movies for style. Veronica Lake's blond tresses, trailing down across one eye, inspired countless women on wartime production lines to wear their hair long and curled at the ends. The U.S. government was eventually forced to ask Paramount Pictures to change her style because so much hair was getting caught in the machinery. Guilaroff's recreation of a nineteenth-century snood for Vivien Leigh in *Gone With the*

Wind inspired thousands of women to pull their hair back in a net, which proved to be better suited to wartime work and austerity.

In Paris, the privations of war challenged every sphere of activity during the Occupation. Fashion, which meant so much to France both culturally and economically, was brought to a near-standstill as most of the fashion houses closed while the occupying forces were in command. But women in the streets showed brave defiance, and the indomitable spirit witnessed by Antoine during the First World War was manifested even more publicly. Women paraded down the avenues in cork-wedge shoes, turbans, and gigantic platter hats decorated with string, wood shavings, recycled trimmings, whatever else was available. During the joyous days after the Liberation, shortages were dealt with as ingeniously as ever: "There is only one hairdresser in all of Paris who can dry your hair: Gervais," reported Lee Miller, the photographer and journalist who

119

Thérèse Chardin,
1965–1966.

arrived with the American troops in 1944. "He has rigged a dryer to his stove pipes which pass through a furnace heated by rubble. The air is sent by fans turned by relay teams of boys riding a stationary tandem bicycle in the basement. They cover 320 kilometers a day to dry 120 heads."[30]

At the same time that Guilaroff was influencing hairstyles via film, the hairdresser Guillaume made an impact by creating coiffures for a great many of the Paris couturiers. He began his long association with the world of couture in the 1930s when he styled pageboys and pin-curled styles for design houses like Vionnet, Mainbocher, and Paquin. He worked through the postwar period, creating the grandiose poufs and sweeping flips that accompanied the looks of Dior, Givenchy, and Balenciaga—Parisian glamour in its most formal evocation. In 1947, Guillaume coiffed the models presenting Christian Dior's landmark "New Look" collection. "I felt that the magnificence of the dresses worn by models, scrupulously chosen for their grace and their natural elegance, was such that the coiffure had to adapt a kind of voluntary effacement," he noted.[31] This masterful yet understated approach served him well. For the next sixteen years, he was entrusted with the top-secret silhouettes at Dior, in order to create hairstyles to complement the fashions. His creations bore poetic names like "*Femme Fleur*," which was shaped to resemble petals blossoming in the sun. Considering that every aspect of the Dior collection, including the coiffure, was immediately copied throughout the world, Guillaume played a major role in transmitting far and wide his idea of French elegance.

Does She or Doesn't She?

Meanwhile, the basic process for haircoloring had not developed much beyond the harsh formulas of previous decades. Vidal Sassoon, who began working in 1942, recalled, "We used to make these diabolical bleaches, mixing twenty-volume peroxide

in a bowl with three drops of ammonia. I had to add the drops, the number had to be exact, and I was terrified my hand would shake—it was as primitive as that."[32] In 1950 only seven percent of American women dyed their hair. Twenty years later, almost seventy percent did.[33] The new acceptance of haircoloring was partly due to the introduction of a single application product, containing both lightener and toner, at a time when more and more women were willing to try home preparations. More significant, however, was the change in attitudes initiated by Clairol's advertising campaign—the provocative "Does She or Doesn't She? . . . Only Her Hairdresser Knows for Sure." This double entendre was pretty heady stuff in the repressive climate of the fifties. The campaign triumphed, making it acceptable to be a "bottle blonde." Fantasy stereotypes such as the fiery, tempestuous redhead played to the lack of fulfillment that many women experienced in the era. Advertising images put women in outfits and

settings that were impossibly glamorous. "Blondes have more fun." Dye your hair and live the fantasy.

The women who dared to color their hair in the fifties did so with a vengeance. A new crop of Hollywood platinum blondes—Marilyn Monroe, Jayne Mansfield, Anita Ekberg—kindled the desire for the ultimate glamour shade, resulting in the industrial-strength bleach jobs of the era. Beauty salons proudly displayed color charts and hair swatches, showing all the vibrant variations made possible by more reliable toners. Names for these hair colors, especially for the Roux brand shades, were a delight: Just Peachy, Bashful Blonde, White Minx, Honey Doux, and the ever-fabulous Frivolous Fawn. A grandmother was no longer simply gray-haired—she could enhance her color with Silver Fox. As more and more women bought into the ritual of haircoloring, salons introduced nuances like frosting or the coloring of individual strands for highlights.

The world was ready for a more indulgent, full-bodied glamour. The Parisian hairdressers

The "Bouffant Belles," an all-girl track team from Abilene, Texas, in a photo taken in 1964 for Sports Illustrated.
One claimed "a bouffant is easier to run in because the wind doesn't blow your hair in your face." Photo Neal Barr, New York.

Mrs. Watson K. Blair.
Hairstyle by Kenneth. Drawing by Henry
Koehler in Vogue, *1963.*

Teenage girls teased and sprayed their hair to amazing extremes. Teachers complained about girls whose hair was so big that students behind them couldn't see the blackboard. Bouffants were so popular that even girls who ran track wore them. In 1964, *Sports Illustrated* devoted a cover story to "Flamin' Mamie's Bouffant Belles," the all-girl Texas Track Club from Abilene. The team's coach, Mamie Ellison, was surely unique in the annals of coaching. Not many other coaches would have had "a can of Rayette's The Young Set hair spray rolling around on the floor of her car."[43] The reporter, Gilbert Rogin, describes Mrs. Ellison as "a 46-year-old divorcée who wears her tinted strawberry blonde hair in what she calls a 'chignon rat.'"[44] In the course of this amazing article, we learn as much about the girls' hair as their track skills: "The Texas Track Team is celebrated on two counts—its athletic achievements and the uncommon beauty of its girls, who compete in dazzling uniforms, elaborate makeup, and majes-

tic hairdos. These hairdos, which are either bouffant or flip if at all possible, may not be aerodynamically sound, and may be 'out' east of the Hudson, but they are an unqualified sensation at a track meet. 'They are our trademark,' says Jeanne Ellison, the coach's 16-year-old daughter. 'A bouffant is easier to run in because the wind doesn't blow your hair in your face.'"[45]

With all the emphasis on setting, women were more dependent than ever on the salon ritual. A *Vogue* article in 1963 entitled "The Kenneth Club" notes, "Women break diets, they skip exercise classes, think nothing of putting off a visit to the dentist. But cancel an appointment with her hairdresser? . . . No smart woman today would dream of it. . . . And possibly not since the Roman baths has there been anything quite like the hairdresser's salon—a place to meet, to see, to be seen, to unwind, to rewind: a part of everyday life.

"No one has more to do with bringing this about in America than Kenneth Battelle. . . . In his

An extraordinary coiffure by Thomas of Michel Kazan, held up with fishing wire for the photo shoot, 1966. Photo Neal Barr, New York.

Coiffure by Alexandre, 1968.
Photo Neal Barr, New York.

hands, hair as wiry and unyielding as a Scotch terrier's coat has been known to swing like velvet."[46] Diana Vreeland was the editor of *Vogue* when the "Kenneth Club" article appeared. In the mid-sixties there were many *Vogue* covers styled by Kenneth with Veruschka and Jean Shrimpton in fantasy styles, including one that incorporated a dozen hairpieces. Vreeland fondly referred to this era as her "Dynel period." She told a story that clearly illustrated her dictum, "if you haven't got it, fake it." For a photo shoot in Tahiti, she came upon the idea of a white horse on the beach, not just any horse, but her romantic fantasy of a horse: "Well, Kenneth was the hairdresser on the Tahiti trip. Some of the great men are hairdressers, and he's the greatest of them. So I said to him, 'The tail of a Tahitian horse may not be . . . enough. You may have to fake it. It may be too skimpy. Best to take along some synthetic hair.' Synthetic hair was better than real hair because you could get as much as you wanted. So we had a horse's

tail made of Dynel for Kenneth to take along just in case. I was in the middle of my Dynel period then—one of the happiest periods of my life, to tell the truth, because I was mad about all the things you could do with Dynel hair. We had the Dynel plaited with bows and bows and bows— these big fat taffeta bows, but rows of them . . . no Infantas ever had it so good!"[47]

   The most influential hairstylists of the day were great believers in wigs and falls for special effects—a high mannerist period in hair design had unfolded. Alexandre, the heir to Antoine and Guillaume as the most celebrated Parisian coiffeur, used hairpieces to style a sea goddess headdress on Marisa Berenson, a fantastic arrangement of seashells, pearls, and coral entwined with fat coils of hair. Neal Barr, a photographer who shot the couture collections for *Harper's Bazaar* in the late sixties, recalled that Alexandre's plentiful use of fake hair made for such heavy arrangements that he often strung invisible

*Nancy Kwan
in Vidal Sassoon's
graduated bob, which
became an international
sensation in 1963.*

wire from the ceiling to steady the precarious piles while they were photographed. Barr, Irving Penn, and other photographers built the models' hair out onto cardboard supports, fanning the real and false hair out across the form and securing it with bobby pins.

Sassoon's Revolution

While synthetic hair dominated as a fantasy look by the 1960s, Kenneth, Alexandre, and Vidal Sassoon all proclaimed the importance of the cut. Hooded dryers were replaced by styling methods using electric rollers, hand-held blow-dryers, and the round brush. But it was Sassoon who made the cut a crusade, and truly a "wash n' blow-dry" revolution. He deplored the artifice he saw while apprenticing in salons: "We'd actually make those rigid curls. I used to look at clients and think, they looked better when they came in!"[48] In 1955 he established his first salon in a walk-up on Bond

Street in London. Even then he emphasized freedom of movement at a time when women did not like to leave the salon without their hair fixed in place. When Sassoon told them, "You don't have to see me for a month," some took it as an affront and others were quite at a loss—this carefree, unfussy approach to styling was too novel.

In 1963, the fashion designer Mary Quant asked him for a modern look to go with the miniskirt. Sassoon's solution would capture the attention of the fashion press worldwide. He told Quant, "I'm going to cut hair like you cut material. No fuss. No ornamentation. Just a neat, clean, swinging line."[49] It was a sensation. In the years that followed, he would introduce an innovation with each fashion season—the "Asymmetric" cut, the "Five Point" cut, always true to his tenets. As his method was based on an individual's bone structure, he encouraged his clients to attain their ideal weight, referring them to fitness programs for health reasons as well as for their self-image.

Sassoon's approach was total care, encompassing lifestyle and fitness; his own line of products followed. The impact was enormous.

As he later recalled, "Fashion had changed, music had changed, the entire culture was in flux, but the hair was still rigid . . . we were creating something that was socially necessary. Women were going back to work, they were assuming their own power. They didn't have time to sit under the dryer anymore."[50]

The international youthquake of the late sixties had a tremendous effect on fashion. Yves Saint Laurent had proclaimed that couture was dead, and Brigitte Bardot said it was for grandmothers—suddenly the handmade, finely-crafted esthetic was replaced by the democratic appeal of mass-produced and secondhand clothing. The civil rights and the women's movements were crucial in forging a counterculture that rejected the materialistic, repressive attitudes of the 1950s. Both women and men let their hair grow long as a

badge of their beliefs. As Graham Nash of the band Crosby, Stills, Nash & Young remembered, "You could see somebody across the street, and if they had long hair, you knew how they thought. You knew that they were into good music. . . . You knew that they probably hated the government. You knew that they probably knew where the best drugs were. . . . And if they had really short hair, you knew what short hair meant. Strange, isn't it?"[51]

HAIR: The American Tribal Love-Rock Musical showed how anarchic reactions to society were embodied in anti-style approachs to hair: "oh say can you see my eyes / if you can / then my hair's too short."[52] Some men adopted long hair as a protest against militarist principles then embodied by the crewcut. Female singers like Janice Joplin flouted conventions that a woman's hair be carefully styled. The Women's Liberation Movement exhorted its followers to shed symbols of repression, be they brassieres or "nice girl" hairbands.

Ruben Toledo drawing of an Afro style.

129

Switched On, *a hairstyle created by Raymond in 1969, inspired by the theme song from* Funny Girl *(left).*

Billboards in American towns read "Beautify America—Get a Haircut!" Young people wore hair that was free and allegedly all-natural, but some women could not resist rolling their hair on orange juice cans for a straighter look; some went so far as to iron it. Black women let their hair grow into Afros and naturals as a symbol of black pride. Wigs crossed racial lines: black women wore blond wigs, while white women wore Afro-textured wigs in black, red, and yellow.

Mohawks and Magenta Hair

In the days of the hippies and after, there was a great demand for natural products and all that was organic was good. Then the punks burst onto the scene in 1976, revelling in shock colors not found in nature—once again, the hair was stripped of its pigment, but this time, the color squeezed from a tube was magenta or acid green. No post-sixties counterculture would pass the worlds of media

and fashion unnoticed, and soon enough the less extreme elements of punk were appropriated into the mainstream. Hair was the most visible part of the rebellious persona. Punks showed that with hair looks, even after the tumultuous styles and anti-styles of the sixties, there were still rules to be broken. They shaved their heads into "mohawks" and sported platinum hair with black roots or vice versa.

In the early days of the trend, when nothing better was available, punks used glue to shape the hair into defiant spikes. Chemists in the haircare companies rushed to develop gels and fixatives that would match glue's bonding power. One of the most enduring punk influences, aside from the music, is a whole range of fixative products initiated by their extreme styles.

As daring as some of the more recent hair trends have been, many have historical precedents. Dollar signs and other symbols shaved into the hair by today's youth are an unmistakable style statement, but artist Man Ray boasted the Surrealist version of the "fade" when he shaved a star onto the back of his head in the 1930s. Runway models with shaved and tattooed heads may seem extreme today, but bald heads stenciled with designs could be found in ancient Rome.

Sassoon's enduring, revolutionary "wash and go" philosophy helped open a new chapter in the history of hairstyles—a history largely filled with aberrations and excess. Over the centuries, hair has been frizzed, teased, padded, coated with lard, drenched with toxic chemicals, and accidentally set on fire—all in the name of beauty. Today's mainstream approach is sensible; style reflects a concern with cut and conditioning. With the nineties came a new wave of natural aids involving aromatherapy—the array of haircare tools offered today is truly dizzying.

Our century has witnessed tremendous advancements. It began with haircare that was similar to that of centuries ago, and is ending with technological breakthroughs that provide precision color, cleansing, and conditioning. Hairstyles have always reflected not only fashion, but women's lives. To think that early in our own century it was scandalous for women to bob their hair! Some women still do schedule weekly salon visits, but it is more a form of indulgence than a prescribed ritual. Fashion has always been a pendulum swinging from one extreme to another, but never has it met with such freedom and power for women to shape their own destinies and appearances. Hair follies such as those presented here may be gone forever, but then again, who can say?

131

The 1980s witnessed another of fashion's cyclical turns toward radical color and eye-catching cuts. High-style punk by Jean-Paul Orsoni, Paris.

Orlando Pita created this hair crown, modeled by Billy Beyond, for the *Love Ball*—a fundraising event on behalf of AIDS research.

•

Mathu & Zaldy styled futuristic, conical curls for the cover of RuPaul's debut recording, "Supermodel of the World," which includes the performer's motto, "Peace, love, and hair grease."

Daring Do's

Marvelous fantasy hair is exceedingly rare these days. For the better part of the twentieth century, common wisdom held that great-looking shoes always hurt and the best hair-styles involved a lot of bother. Fashion was a world in which the look was delivered from on high, never mind tedious details like comfort and practicality. But the attitude today is decidedly different. High-style hairdressing has been marginalized, certainly in women's day-to-day lives, and even in the fashion magazines, a realm in which fantasy concepts have traditionally flourished. There is little stress to be had in today's minimalist approach to hair, except for the $200 pricetag that comes with a cut at a top salon.

Given the predominance of unstartling hair, it is all the more eye-popping when a magazine spread or fashion runway, a music video or a film, serves up a look that is completely over the top: like the wig Debbie Harry

Debbie Harry in John Waters's *Hairspray*.

133

For New York City's
downtown diva
Susanne Bartsch,
Danilo created one of
the hair constructions
he calls his
"hieroglyphic towers."
There is no wire
support—the edifice is
made completely from
gelatinized hair.

Two styles showing the tremendous variety among hairstyles for black women. Above: an elaborately threaded hairstyle by Veron Charles of Harlem, NY. Below: an "African Pride" hair creation by Sally Kamara and Joan Gardner of MJ's Unisex, Queens, NY.

wore in the John Waters film Hairspray—so big that it concealed a bomb. Or drag superstar / recording artist RuPaul's hair extravaganza video Back to my Roots, which passes judgement on a parade of black hair trends and products: "jheri-curl, afro-puffs, banji girls." New York's annual Wigstock festival provides a yearly shot of hair-wildness, fierce and funny, ignoring for the most part whatever may be the mainstream currents in fashion.

One of the few contexts in which elaborate hairdressing remains fashionable is in the realm of African-inspired styles. Black women and men throughout the world are reinterpreting these intricate traditional styles, decorating tiny plaits with beads and cowrie shells, or simply finding inspiration in the sculptural qualities of the hair itself. Astonishing hairstyles are created for evenings out, but the looks are not limited to special occasions—they can be seen on the job or on the street. Besides preserving methods of African hairdressing that are at least three thousand years old, black women are carrying forward

Right: The Chanel logo wrapped in hair. This headdress from the Wigstock 1992 festival has the size and artistry an 18th-century lady might admire.

Julien d'Ys styled massive wigs for Karl Lagerfeld's Fall 1994 collection that suggested a hybrid of an 18th-century powdered *tour* and dreadlocks. Makeup by Stephane Marais. Model: Christian.

A faux-chignon shown with Christian Lacroix's 1988 couture collection (above). A style from the Veiled Goddess wedding series by Ruth Sinclair af the Khamit Kinks salon in Atlanta (right). John D'Orazio's "Ocean Fantasy" required days of construction, starting with the wire armature and finishing with shell-encrusted nets woven from hair. Mermaids by Susan Snodgrass and Stephanie Blythe (below).

another age-old tradition: that of the lingering and social toilette. The time-consuming plaiting and threading is carried out in a salon, or friends and relatives work on each other's hair, now and then taking days to complete a full, minutely-worked "African Temple" or "Senegalese Twist."

Since hair artistry is usually so fleeting, the fantastic styles on these pages have been captured for more enduring appreciation. Most of the looks were created especially for this book. These remarkable styles prove that the irresistible urge to create Daring Do's surfaces even in the most sensible times.

Notes

INTRODUCTION
1. Beverley Nichols, *The Sweet and Twenties* (London: Weidenfeld and Nicholson, 1958), p. 135.
2. Roger Lonsdale, ed., *The New Oxford Book of Eighteenth Century Verse* (Oxford: Oxford University Press, 1992), p. 92.
3. William Kingsley, *Context 2: Rape of the Lock* (Hamden, CT: Archon Books, 1977), p. 1.
4. Lonsdale, op. cit., p. 96.
5. Ovid, *The Erotic Poems*, trans. Peter Green (London: Penguin, 1982), p. 182.
6. Ibid., p. 95.
7. Frances Mossiker, *Madame de Sévigné. A Life and Letters* (New York: Knopf, 1983), p. 103.
8. Antoine, *Antoine by Antoine* (London: W.H. Allen, 1946), p. 120.
9. Alexandre quoted in American *Vogue*, "The History of the Hairdresser," July 1990, p. 83.

ANCIENT ARTIFICE
1. Brooks Adams and David Revere McFadden, *Hair* (New York: Cooper-Hewitt Museum, 1980), p. 26.
2. Mila Contini, *Fashion from Ancient Egypt to the Present Day* (London: Paul Hamlyn, 1967), p. 22.
3. Wendy Cooper, *Hair: Sex Society Symbolism* (New York: Stein and Day, 1971), p. 121.
4. Rita E. Freed, an entry on wigs in *Egypt's Golden Age: The Art of Living in the New Kingdom 1558–1085 B.C.*, ed. Edward Brovarski (Boston: Museum of Fine Arts, 1982), p. 196.
5. M. Gaultier-Laurent, *Les Scenes de Coiffure Feminine dans l'ancienne Egypte.* (Institut Francais d'Archaeologie, 1938), p. 680.
6. Diane Ackerman, *A Natural History of the Senses* (New York: Random House, 1991), p. 51.
7. Ibid.
8. Gay Robins, *Women in Ancient Egypt* (Cambridge, MA: Harvard University Press, 1993), p. 51.
9. Ibid., p. 50.
10. Meleager, "Heliodora's Wreath" in *The Penguin Book of Greek Verse*, ed. Constantine A. Trypanis (London: Penguin, 1971), p. 348.
11. Anacreon, "The Motley-sandalled Girl," ibid., p. 157.
12. Menander cited in Charles Panati, *Extraordinary Origins of Everyday Things* (New York: Harper & Row, 1987), p. 231.
13. Cooper, op. cit., p. 123.
14. Ruth Turner Wilcox, *The Modes in Hats and Headdress, including hairstyles, cosmetics, and jewelry* (New York: Charles Scribner's and Sons, 1959), p. 20.
15. Ovid, op. cit., p. 218.
16. Juvenal cited in Jerome Carcopino, *Daily Life in Ancient Rome* (New Haven: Yale University Press, 1968), p. 168.
17. Ovid, op. cit., p. 182.

18. Carcopino, op. cit., p. 168.
19. Ibid.
20. Ovid, op. cit., p. 221.
21. Ibid., pp. 107–109.
22. [Anonymous], "The Description of Chrysorrhoe," Trypanis, op. cit., p. 447.
23. Mary Rogers, "The decorum of women's beauty: Trissino, Firenzuola, Luigini and the representation of women in sixteenth-century painting" *Renaissance Studies*, vol. 2, no. 1 (Oxford: Oxford University Press, Society for Renaissance Studies, 1988), p. 62.
24. Agnolo Firenzuola, *Of the Beauty of Women*, trans. Clara Bell (London: James Osgood, 1892), pp. 79, 107.
25. Christopher Hare, *The Most Illustrious Ladies of the Italian Renaissance* (New York: Charles Scribner's Sons, 1904), p. 273.
26. Rogers, op. cit., p. 63.
27. Firenzuola, op. cit., p. 123.
28. Cited in Janet Arnold, ed., *Queen Elizabeth's Wardrobe Unlocked* (London: Maney, 1988), p. 110.
29. Foley's comments from "Records of the English Province of the Society of Jesus" cited in Jane Asheford, *Dress in the Age of Elizabeth I* (London: Batsford, 1988), p. 4.

A GALLERY OF EXTRAVAGANCES
1. From an English engraving in the coiffure volumes of the Maciet collection (vol. 218, no. 4) at the Bibliothèque des Arts Décoratifs, Paris.
2. Nina Epton, *Love and the French* (Cleveland: World Publishing Company, 1959), p. 19.
3. Vita Sackville-West, *Daughter of France: The Life of La Grande Mademoiselle* (Garden City, NY: Doubleday, 1959), p. 193.
4. de Réaux cited in G. d'Eze and A. Marcel, *Histoire de la coiffure des femmes en france* (Paris: Paul Ollendorf, 1886), p. 112.
5. Mossiker, op. cit., pp. 103–104.
6. Diana de Marly, *Louis XIV and Versailles* (London: Batsford, 1987), p. 79.
7. Thomas Hall, B.D. and Pastor of Kings Norton, *The Loathesomeness of Long Haire . . . With an Appendix against Painting, Spots, Naked Breasts, etc.* (London: Nathaniel Webb and William Grantham, 1654), from the unpaginated introduction.
8. Panati, op. cit., p. 236.
9. Ibid., p. 224.
10. de Marly, op. cit., p. 93.
11. Ibid., p. 123.
12. d'Eze and Marcel, op. cit., p. 133.
13. de Marly, op. cit., p. 125.
14. Arthur R. Ropes, ed., *Mary Wortley Montagu written by Herself*, from the "Beaux and Belles of England" series (New York: Athenaeum Press, n.d. circa 1930), p. 78.
15. Ibid.
16. Karl Toth, *Woman and Rococo in France* (London: George Harrap, 1931), p. 319.
17. Cooper, op. cit., p. 95.
18. Neville Williams, *Powder and Paint: A History of the Englishwoman's Toilet* (London: Longmans, Green and Co., 1957), p. 89.
19. Cooper, op. cit., p. 95.
20. Ibid.
21. Eleanor Farjeon, *The New Book of Days* (New York: Walck, 1961), p. 100.
22. Williams, op. cit., p. 63.
23. Legros de Rumigny recipe cited in Richard Corson, *Fashions in Hair: The First Five Thousand Years* (London: Peter Owen, 1965), p. 332.
24. Peter Gilchrist, *A Treatise on the Hair or Every Lady her own Hair-Dresser* (London: by the author, n.d. circa 1770), p. 10.
25. Ibid., p. 4.
26. l'Ecole de Salerne, *l'Art de Conserver sa Santé, Augmenté d'un Traité sur la Conservation de la Beauté des Dames, et de Plusiers autres Secrets utiles et agréables* (Paris: La Compagnie des Libraires, 1766), p. 135.
27. Gilchrist, op. cit., p. 4.
28. Ibid., p. 1.
29. Ibid., p. 13.
30. Nancy Mitford, *Madame de Pompadour* (New York: E.P. Dutton, 1984), p. 39.
31. Stefan Zweig, *Marie Antoinette: The Portrait of an Average Woman* (New York: Garden City Publishing, 1933), p. 95.
32. Olivier Bernier, *Pleasure and Privilege: Life in France, Naples, and America 1770–1790* (New York: Doubleday, 1981), p. 74.
33. Zweig, op. cit., p. 96.
34. Ibid., p. 97.
35. Paul Lesniewicz, *The World of Bonsai* (London: Blanford, 1990), p. 31.
36. Claude-Anne Lopez, *Mon Cher Papa: Franklin and the Ladies of Paris* (New Haven: Yale University Press), p. 203.

37. La Marquise de la Tour du Pin, *Recollections of the Revolution and the Empire*, Walter Geer, trans. (New York: Brentano's, 1920), p. 51.
38. Muriel Masefield, ed., *The Diary and Letters of Madame d'Arblay (Frances Burney)* (New York: E.P. Dutton, 1931), p. 44.
39. Ibid., p. 139.
40. Fanny Burney, *Evelina* (New York: Signet Classics, 1992), p. 26.
41. de la Tour du Pin, op. cit., p. 65.
42. Aileen Ribeiro, *Dress in Eighteenth-century Europe 1715–1789* (London: Batsford, 1984), pp. 159–160.
43. James Laver, *Clothes* (New York: Horizon Press, 1953), p. 184.
44. Bernier, op. cit., p. 78.
45. James Reynolds, *Baroque Splendour* (New York: Creative Age, 1950), p. 63.
46. Ribeiro, op. cit., p. 87.
47. Bernier, op. cit., p. 77.
48. Epton, op. cit., p. 204.
49. Cooper, op. cit., p. 95.
50. Zweig, op. cit., p. 368.

TOUSLED TRESSES AND CORKSCREW CURLS
1. General Fleishmann, ed. *Memoirs of Count Miot de Melito* (New York: Charles Scribner's Sons, 1881), p. 132.
2. Ibid., p. 131.
3. Aileen Ribeiro, *Fashion in the French Revolution* (London: Batsford, 1988), p. 124.
4. d'Eze and Marcel, op. cit., p. 227.
5. Ibid.
6. Ibid., p. 229.
7. *Journal des Dames et des Modes* (4 March 1798), fashion plate in Ribeiro, op. cit, p. 96.
8. John Canaday, *Mainstreams of Modern Art* (New York: Simon and Schuster, 1959), p. 20.
9. Laver, op. cit., p. 185.
10. Honoré de Balzac, "Domestic Peace" in *Selected Short Stories* (London: Penguin, 1977), p. 29.
11. Angus Holden, *Elegant Modes in the Nineteenth Century from High Waist to Bustle* (London: George Allen, 1935), p. 20.
12. Michele Majer, essay in *The Age of Napoleon* (New York: Metropolitan Museum of Art, 1989), p. 234.
13. Ibid., p. 230.
14. Ibid.
15. Arthur Sheehan and Elizabeth Odell, *Black Pearl:*

The Hairdresser from Haiti (London: Harvill, 1956), p. 200.
16. Ibid., p. 63.
17. Octave Uzanne, *The Frenchwoman in the Century* (New York: George Routledge, 1887), pp. 120–121.
18. Gilbert Foan, *The Art and Craft of Hairdressing* (London: New Era, n.d. circa 1935), p. 178.
19. Professeur Croisat, *Les Cent-Un Coiffeurs de tous les Pays* (Paris: 1836), p. 109.
20. Ibid., p. 13.
21. Ibid., p. 14.
22. Ibid., p. 93.
23. Ibid., p. 92.
24. Ibid., p. 109.
25. Uzanne, op. cit., p. 166.
26. Ibid, p. 125.
27. Charlotte Brontë, *Jane Eyre* (London: Penguin, 1985), p. 79.
28. Jean Keyes, *A History of Women's Hairstyles 1500–1965* (London: Methuen Co., 1967), p. 41.
29. Laver, op. cit., p. 201.
30. Ibid, pp. 186–187.
31. C. Willett Cunnington cited in Laver, ibid., p. 187.
32. Ibid., p. 31.
33. Rita Wellman, *Victoria Royal. The Flowering of a Style* (New York: Scribner's 1939), pp. 106–107.
34. Mark Campbell, *The Art of Hair Work. Hair Braiding and Jewelry of Sentiment with a Catalog of Hair Jewelry*. reprint eds. Jules and Kaethe Kliot. (Berkeley, CA: Lacis Publications, 1994), p. 197.
35. Honoré de Balzac "Autre étude de femme" in *Les Secrets de la Princesse de Cadignan et autre études de femme* (Paris: Gallimard, 1980), p. 55.
36. Wellman, op cit., p. 25.
37. Lynn Yaeger, "Hair Jewelry," *The Village Voice*, 28 March, 1989, p. 41.
38. J. Stevens Cox, *An Illustrated Dictionary of Hairdressing and Wigmaking* (London: Hairdresser's Technical Council, 1966), p. 89.
39. Laver, op cit., p. 181.
40. Ibid., p. 192.
41. Phillis Cunnington, *Costume in Pictures* (London: Studio Vista Ltd., 1964), p. 149.
42. Keyes, op. cit., p. 47.
43. Cox, op. cit., p. 32.
44. Laver, op. cit., p. 197.
45. Cooper, op. cit., p. 28.

46. Marcel Proust, *Remembrance of Things Past* (New York: Random House, 1934), trans. C. K. Scott Moncrieff, p. 742.
47. Ibid., p. 751.
48. Ibid.
49. Uzanne, op cit., pp. 241–242.
50. Laver, op. cit., p. 189.

BOBS, BEEHIVES, AND BLONDES
1. Antoine, op. cit., p. 25.
2. Mary Elizabeth Edes and Dudley Frazier, eds., *The Age of Extravagance: An Edwardian Reader* (New York: Rinehart, 1954), p. 128.
3. Ella Adelia Fletcher, *The Woman Beautiful* (New York: Brentano's, 1901), p. 254.
4. Ibid., p. 261.
5. Ibid., pp. 261–62.
6. Ibid., p. 260.
7. Adams and McFadden, op. cit., p. 19.
8. Panati, op. cit., pp. 236–37.
9. Antoine, op. cit., p. 77.
10. Ibid., p. 78.
11. Palmer White, *Elsa Schiaparelli: Empress of Paris Fashion* (New York: Rizzoli, 1986), p. 101.
12. Antoine, op. cit., p. 86.
13. Ibid., p. 75.
14. Valerie Steele, *Paris Fashion: A Cultural History* (New York: Oxford University Press, 1988), p. 264.
15. David Chierichetti, "Short Hair Styles of the 20's Bob-Bobbing Along—Again," *Los Angeles Times*, 23 August 1985, Part V, p. 1.
16. Antoine, op. cit., p. 79.
17. Cited in Neville Williams, *Powder and Paint: A History of the Englishwoman's Toilet* (London: Longmans, Green & Company, 1957), pp. 162–63.
18. Chierichetti, op. cit., p. 12.
19. F. Scott Fitzgerald, *The Stories of F. Scott Fitzgerald* (New York: Macmillan Publishing, 1986), p. 57.
20. Gilbert A. Foan, *The Art and Craft of Hairdressing* (London: New Era, n.d. circa 1935), p. 310.
21. Ibid.
22. Williams, op. cit., p. 123.
23. Brassaï, *The Secret Paris of the 30's* (New York: Pantheon Books, 1976), [from the unpaginated section on *The Bals-Musette*].
24. Antoine, op. cit., p. 120.
25. Ibid., p. 123.
26. "The New Feeling of Femininity goes to the Head of the Mode," American *Vogue*, 1 February 1928, p. 75.
27. Clifton Fadiman, ed., *Profiles from the New Yorker* (New York: Knopf, 1938), p. 246.
28. Foan, op. cit., p. 364.
29. Conversation with my mother, May 1994.
30. Joan Kron, "When Beauty was a Duty," *New York Times*, 8 February 1991, Section C, p. 1.
31. Guillaume, *Guillaume raconte . . . la coiffure et ses metamorphoses* (Paris: Guillaume, 1982), p. 77.
32. Georgina Howell, "The Big Shear," American *Vogue*, January 1993, p. 84.
33. Panati, op. cit., p. 233.
34. Christophe Carita and Denise Dubois-Jallais, *Carita Saga* (Paris: Carita, S.A, 1988), pp. 53–54.
35. Ibid., p. 58.
36. Ibid.
37. Ibid., p. 112.
38. Ibid.
39. Shirley Lord, ed., beauty column in American *Vogue*, March 1990, p. 264.
40. Cox, op. cit., p. 9.
41. Ackerman, op. cit., p. 86.
42. Conversation with Orlando Pita, New York City, July 1993.
43. Gilbert Rogin, "Flamin' Mamie's Bouffant Belles: A beauty-minded Texan pioneers a few glamorous looks in women's track." *Sports Illustrated*, 20 April 1964, p. 30.
44. Ibid.
45. Ibid.
46. "The Kenneth Club" (unsigned) article in American *Vogue*, July 1963, p. 52.
47. Diana Vreeland, *DV* (New York: Vintage Books, 1985), pp. 200–01.
48. Diane Fishman and Marcia Powell, *Vidal Sassoon. Fifty Years Ahead* (New York: Rizzoli, 1993), p. 30.
49. Ibid., p. 74.
50. Paddy Calistro, "The Man Behind Wash'n'Wear Hair," *Los Angeles Times*, 26 February 1993, Section E, p. 1.
51. *Making Sense of the Sixties* transcript #3, p. 1, television broadcast aired on WNET, New York, 22 January 1991.
52. Jerome Ragni and James Rado, *HAIR: The American Tribal Love-Rock Musical* (New York: Pocket Books, 1970), p. 65.

Index

A flamboyant hair creation by Kerry Warn topped with burning candles.